Praise for *Marketing Lessons from the Grateful Dead*

"Scott and Halligan have written one of the most inspired, practical, and unconventional books on the business bookshelf. Want to develop a cult-like following, establish a new category, and do what you love? Scott and Halligan—calling upon their innate marketing savvy and inspired by their passion for the Grateful Dead—show you how."

—Marc Benioff, Chairman and CEO, Salesforce.com

"Demand everything. Expect nothing."

—Bill Kreutzmann, cofounder and drummer, the Grateful Dead

"I miss Jerry. And I wonder . . . is your brand iconic? Why not? Hint: It has nothing whatsoever to do with hemp brownies. Becoming iconic is a choice."

—Seth Godin, author of *Linchpin*; blogger; Deadhead

"For years, business theorists and corporate strategists have pointed to the Dead's example for insights into perennial issues and emerging challenges. Scott and Halligan focus on one key factor in the band's extraordinary artistic and business success—their iconic and enduring identity, not just as a band but as a brand. The authors' real appreciation for the Dead phenomenon, and their compelling and creative analyses of the Dead's marketing acumen, make this thought-provoking survey mandatory reading."

—Nicholas Meriwether, Grateful Dead Archivist, University of California, Santa Cruz, and author of *All Graceful Instruments: The Contexts of the Grateful Dead Phenomenon* and *Dead Letters: Essays on the Grateful Dead*

"Jerry Garcia and his band were brilliant marketers. They understood that you grow your fan base one fan at a time, and they constantly came up with things to energize their base while continuing to build it. As committed fans and talented marketing pros, Brian and David have created a book that is both entertaining and informative."

—Jim Irsay, Owner and CEO, Indianapolis Colts and owner of Jerry Garcia's guitar, Tiger

"David and Brian share my deep passion for music and its inspiration in our everyday lives. In *Marketing Lessons from the Grateful Dead*, they combine their marketing expertise with a zeal for one of the most successful and iconic bands of all time. They mold two subjects that are seemingly poles apart into one breakthrough book that is as entertaining as it is enlightening."

—Del Breckenfeld, Director, Entertainment Marketing, Fender Musical Instruments Corp. and author of *The Cool Factor: Building Your Brand's Image Through Partnership Marketing*

"*Marketing Lessons from the Grateful Dead* explores the phenomenon created by the Grateful Dead showcasing the extraordinary power of music and the innovations the Dead developed to connect and bond with their audience."

—Michael Lang, Co-Creator and Producer of the 1969 Woodstock Music & Art Festival and author of *The Road to Woodstock*

Also by Brian Halligan

Inbound Marketing: *Attract, Engage, and Delight Customers Online*
(with Dharmesh Shah)

Also by David Meerman Scott

The New Rules of Marketing & PR: *How to Use Content Marketing, AI, Social Media, Podcasting, Video, and Newsjacking to Reach Buyers Directly*

Fanocracy: *Turning Fans into Customers and Customers into Fans (with Reiko Scott)*

Standout Virtual Events: *How to create an experience that your audience will love* (with Michelle Manafy)

Marketing the Moon: *The Selling of the Apollo Lunar Program* (with Richard Jurek)

The New Rules of Sales & Service: *How to Use Agile Selling, Real-Time Customer Engagement, Big Data, Content, and Storytelling to Grow Your Business*

World Wide Rave: *Creating Triggers That Get Millions of People to Spread Your Ideas and Share Your Stories*

Tuned In: *Uncover the Extraordinary Opportunities That Lead to Business Breakthroughs*
(with Craig Stull and Phil Myers)

Cashing In with Content: *How Innovative Marketers Use Digital Information to Turn Browsers into Buyers*

Eyeball Wars: *A Novel of Dot-Com Intrigue*

Marketing Lessons from The Grateful Dead

WHAT EVERY BUSINESS CAN LEARN FROM THE MOST ICONIC BAND IN HISTORY

Brian Halligan
David Meerman Scott

Foreword by
Bill Walton

WILEY

Copyright © 2010, revised 2026 by Brian Halligan and David Merman Scott. All rights reserved.

Published by John Wiley & Sons, Inc., Hoboken, New Jersey.
Published simultaneously in Canada.

No part of this publication may be reproduced, stored in a retrieval system, or transmitted in any form or by any means, electronic, mechanical, photocopying, recording, scanning, or otherwise, except as permitted under Section 107 or 108 of the 1976 United States Copyright Act, without either the prior written permission of the Publisher, or authorization through payment of the appropriate per-copy fee to the Copyright Clearance Center, Inc., 222 Rosewood Drive, Danvers, MA 01923, (978) 750-8400, fax (978) 750-4470, or on the web at www.copyright.com. Requests to the Publisher for permission should be addressed to the Permissions Department, John Wiley & Sons, Inc., 111 River Street, Hoboken, NJ 07030, (201) 748-6011, fax (201) 748-6008, or online at http://www.wiley.com/go/permission.

The manufacturer's authorized representative according to the EU General Product Safety Regulation is Wiley-VCH GmbH, Boschstr. 12, 69469 Weinheim, Germany, e-mail: Product_Safety@wiley.com.

This publication has not been approved, sponsored, or licensed by the Grateful Dead.

Trademarks: Wiley and the Wiley logo are trademarks or registered trademarks of John Wiley & Sons, Inc. and/or its affiliates in the United States and other countries and may not be used without written permission. All other trademarks are the property of their respective owners. John Wiley & Sons, Inc. is not associated with any product or vendor mentioned in this book.

Limit of Liability/Disclaimer of Warranty: While the publisher and the authors have used their best efforts in preparing this work, including a review of the content of the work, neither the publisher nor the authors make any representations or warranties with respect to the accuracy or completeness of the contents of this work and specifically disclaim all warranties, including without limitation any implied warranties of merchantability or fitness for a particular purpose. No warranty may be created or extended by sales representatives, written sales materials or promotional statements for this work. The fact that an organization, website, or product is referred to in this work as a citation and/or potential source of further information does not mean that the publisher and authors endorse the information or services the organization, website, or product may provide or recommendations it may make. This work is sold with the understanding that the publisher is not engaged in rendering professional services. The advice and strategies contained herein may not be suitable for your situation. You should consult with a specialist where appropriate. Further, readers should be aware that websites listed in this work may have changed or disappeared between when this work was written and when it is read. Neither the publisher nor authors shall be liable for any loss of profit or any other commercial damages, including but not limited to special, incidental, consequential, or other damages.

For general information on our other products and services or for technical support, please contact our Customer Care Department within the United States at (800) 762-2974, outside the United States at (317) 572-3993 or fax (317) 572-4002.

Wiley also publishes its books in a variety of electronic formats. Some content that appears in print may not be available in electronic formats. For more information about Wiley products, visit our web site at www.wiley.com.

Library of Congress Cataloging-in-Publication Data is Available:

ISBN 9781394378012 (Paper)
ISBN 9780470900529 (Cloth)
ISBN 9780470940846 (ePub)
ISBN 9780470940938 (ePDF)

Cover Design: Wiley
Cover Images: © mecaleha/Getty Images,
© Man_Half-tube/Getty Images
Back Cover Photograph: © Jay Blakesberg/Retro Photo Archive

SKY10127792_100325

The Grateful Dead was always known for generosity and the performance of numerous benefit concerts.

In this spirit, the authors are donating 100 percent of the profits from this book to The Grateful Guitars Foundation.

Grateful Guitars is a 501-c3 nonprofit that supports music instruction in schools to seed the next generations of musicians.

We also acquire world-class musical instruments for talented players who seek to carry on the tradition of jam band music into the 21st century and beyond. Through the powerful connection between skilled players and the highest quality instruments, our aim is to ensure that jam band music thrives decades into the future. Additionally, Grateful Guitars Foundation board members share Grateful Dead stage used instruments and gear from their personal collections with musicians who focus on Grateful Dead music.

www.gratefulguitars.org

Contents

FOREWORD	xi
INTRODUCTION TO THE ORIGINAL EDITION	xv
PREFACE	xxvii

PART ONE	**THE BAND**	1
Chapter 1	Create a Unique Business Model	3
Chapter 2	Choose Memorable Brand (and Band) Names	13
Chapter 3	Build a Diverse Team	21
Chapter 4	Be Yourself	29
Chapter 5	Experiment, Experiment, Experiment	37
Chapter 6	Embrace Technology	45
Chapter 7	Establish a New Category	53
PART TWO	**THE FANS**	59
Chapter 8	Encourage Eccentricity	61
Chapter 9	Bring People on an Odyssey	69
Chapter 10	Put Fans in the Front Row	79
Chapter 11	Build a Following	87
PART THREE	**THE BUSINESS**	95
Chapter 12	Cut Out the Middleman	97
Chapter 13	Free Your Content	105
Chapter 14	Be Spreadable	113
Chapter 15	Upgrade to Premium	119
Chapter 16	Loosen Up Your Brand	127
Chapter 17	Partner with Entrepreneurs	135
Chapter 18	Give Back	143
Chapter 19	Do What You Love	151

Acknowledgments	157
"Furthur" Reading	159
About the Photographs	161
About the Illustrations	161
About the Authors	163

Foreword

More than 60 years ago a bunch of young guys in the San Francisco Bay Area, living in their cars and on tomato soup made from tap water and ketchup packages lifted from fast-food restaurants, had a dream and vision of driving the train that would change our world on so many fronts.

That band of merry pranksters ultimately became the Grateful Dead. They have changed the way we live and think—in ways we don't even know. But of all the lasting impact that they have bestowed upon us, who would have ever thought that it would be their business and marketing models that would today be the envy of the culture that they all fought so hard to change.

And now a couple of young scientists, economists and historians, true new-age Cosmic Charlies—Brian Halligan and David Meerman Scott—have help on the way. They have come up with a fascinating story of how the Grateful Dead's counter-intuitive ways of doing business are really best business practices that work for everyone.

Brian and David's newest book, *Marketing Lessons from the Grateful Dead*, is like a powerful, hard-charging anthem that fills in so many blanks while closing the circle of life all around us. Like the Grateful Dead, Brian and David are transformational visionaries with a keen eye for the second set.

Their ability to synthesize the core values, beliefs, and best practices of the Grateful Dead are captured brilliantly in a thoroughly enjoyable and readily applicable package that is like the release of the band's next album—eagerly anticipated by all.

Like other daring visionaries, the Grateful Dead rejected conventional wisdom. They had a willingness and confidence to take a chance on something new and different. They cut themselves loose from their fear of failure and the unknown. They worked and they played on the edge, and did both loud, fast, and free of traditional constraints.

Their passion, creative spirit, imaginative soul, and industrious commitment to promote truth, fairness, justice, and the Grateful Dead way led them through the evolutionary transition where they went from playing for silver to playing for life. This book tells you how to make that transition for your own career.

In the band's never-ending battle against the dire wolves of deceit and false prophets (and profits), the Grateful Dead—a shining star, a beacon of hope on a bleak landscape—have been able to rise above the blinding madness with innovative promotional techniques, viral marketing, a commitment to customer service, personalized ticket and merchandising plans, and a sense of community and team that was unheard of years ago, but is clearly now the standard new path to the promised land. It all seems so simple—yet so frustratingly elusive. We all have two eyes, but still some of us can't see.

In life, we get rare opportunities to climb aboard a new bus heading down the road to where the water tastes like wine. Brian and David are today's newest chauffeurs. They have given us a fresh and delicious chance to get it done—and we might as well.

Like the Grateful Dead, they epitomize the mantra from so many roads traveled blindly, with little more than faith—"We sure don't know what we're going for—but we're going to go for it for sure."

And that is why after gleefully consuming *Marketing Lessons from the Grateful Dead* and following these guys who have done so well by doing good, I stand tall and proud in my choice, satisfied with my willing sacrifice, and happy with my undying love and loyalty, while forever waving that flag, and singing loudly, "I'm with those guys."

Marketing? The Grateful Dead? Who would have ever thought?

Once in a while you get shown the light, in the strangest of places if you look at it right . . .

—Bill Walton, basketball legend and Deadhead

Introduction to the original edition

"THERE IS NOTHING LIKE A GRATEFUL DEAD CONCERT"
First used in the liner notes of the Grateful Dead album *Europe '72*.

Picture a summer evening, and imagine that you are in a sold-out arena. The audience members have been partying all afternoon in the hot sunshine, hanging with old friends, meeting new ones, drinking, laughing, smoking....

The collective anticipation in the arena feels positively electric, enhanced by the sounds from the stage, which hums with tens of thousands of watts of pure power ready to rock. The house lights go down and a cheer goes up. Hundreds of tiny red lights on the band's onstage equipment are visible, blinking on and off like fireflies as the musicians shuffle onto the stage.

Phil Lesh, Bob Weir, and Jerry Garcia plug in and noodle around a bit on their guitars, their backs to the audience. The two drummers settle in behind their kits. One sends out a cosmic *boom* from a bass drum, and we in the audience feel it as much as we hear it. A cheer for the *boom*! Some people try to discern what song the band will open with, based on the quasi-riffs now being played. Set-list savants predict the opener to their friends, based on the algorithms they used that morning to query databases of every song ever played by the band. Then quietly, slowly at first, the band coalesces around a familiar tune. They turn to face the crowd. The lights come up. The volume is cranked. And 20,000 people collectively begin to boogie. Another Grateful Dead concert has left the station.

The Grateful Dead emerged out of San Francisco in 1965, during an exceptional period in American history. The Vietnam War was escalating and the civil rights movement was in full swing. Young people were beginning to question authority in large numbers, and the counterculture scene was growing. The band grew in popularity during the late 1960s, releasing their first album in 1967 and playing Woodstock in 1969. But unlike many other bands that faded away or broke up, the Grateful Dead played on into the 1970s, 1980s, and 1990s, with band members continuing to play together today, gaining new fans along the way, including us.

We decided to take our fandom to a new level and write about the Grateful Dead. However, we're certainly not the first people to identify the Grateful Dead as a band worthy of study. In the past few years, a wave of interest in the band has emerged in a wide variety of fields.

A conference at the University of Massachusetts at Amherst called "Unbroken Chain: The Grateful Dead in Music, Culture and Memory" brought together scholars, fans, artists, performers and members of the extended Grateful Dead family for the first major university conference on the enduring legacy of the Grateful Dead experience. The conference included more than 50 presenters in 20 panel

Introduction to the original edition

discussions ranging from music composition and improvisation to an examination of the band's business model. There were musical performances, gallery exhibits, and presentations; and the conference served to legitimize the study of the band. Brian attended the conference and it got his mind spinning about the possibilities of the band as a marketing example.

Then in 2009, the University of California at Santa Cruz acquired the Grateful Dead archive, considered one of the most significant collections of twentieth century American popular culture. The archive includes 600,000 linear feet of books, recordings, business correspondence, posters, tickets, photographs, films, stage props, and more. The acquisition prompted excitement from scholars in many disciplines eager to gain inside knowledge for their work in sociology, history, art, musicology, and business theory—both within and beyond the Grateful Dead community.

In March 2010, the New York Historical Society opened the first large-scale exhibition of materials from the Grateful Dead Archive. "Grateful Dead: Now Playing at the New York Historical Society" chronicled the history of the band, its music, and the phenomenal longevity of the Grateful Dead community through original art and documents related to the band, its members, performances, and productions. We were both thrilled to participate in a private tour of the exhibition led by Grateful Dead drummer Bill Kreutzmann. The exhibit, which ran through July 2010, explored, in part, the band's refusal to follow established music industry rules.

It is this marketing savvy, including direct contact with fans, a focus on touring, and other innovations that we profile in detail within these pages.

So, why all the fuss?

Well, the Grateful Dead played over 2,300 live concerts from 1965 to 1995, establishing the band as the most popular touring act in rock history. While the band also saw success with 13 studio albums, it was the live concert experience that set them apart. The Grateful Dead created a free-form live sound that combined elements of many different musical styles (rock, country-western, improvisational jazz, gospel, and more) to create a completely new and unique sound. The band played about 500 songs live over a 30-year career, and of those 150 were original compositions. The band covered songs from such diverse artists as Bob Dylan ("All Along the Watchtower"), Kris Kristofferson ("Me and Bobby McGee"), Johnny Cash ("Big River"), Steve Winwood ("Dear Mr. Fantasy"), Chuck Berry ("Johnny B. Goode"), and The Beatles ("Day Tripper"). Unlike most rock acts that played the same songs in the same order every show, you never knew what Grateful Dead you would get in a given night, and that surprise element was part of the Grateful Dead experience.

A Grateful Dead concert was more than just . . . well . . . a concert. It was a happening, a destination, and, for the most diehard fans, it was their lives. Indeed, some people followed the band from city to city, attending each of the roughly 100 shows that they played in a typical year. Many supported themselves by selling goods—food, drink, drugs, or Grateful Dead–themed merchandise—in the parking lot "scene" at each venue.

Grateful Dead shows were a place where people bonded. The traveling caravan was a true community—a collaboration between the fans and the band—providing "Deadheads" with a sense of belonging (as well as some damned fine music). The concert experience was a counterculture adventure and many people treated the shows as a pilgrimage. Inside the arenas 20,000 fans would come together as one organism, bonding in a way not unlike that seen in a religious movement.

MARKETING LESSONS

In the 1960s the Grateful Dead pioneered many social media and inbound marketing concepts that businesses across all industries use today. The band made a series of difficult and often unpopular decisions in order to differentiate themselves from their competition by providing the highest quality service to their fans. They were not simply selling a product. The Dead pioneered a "freemium" business model, allowing concert attendees to record and trade concert tapes, building a powerful word-of-mouth fan network powered by free music. Instead of obsessing over recording, the Dead became the most popular touring band of their era, selling hundreds of millions of dollars' worth of tickets, and creating a highly profitable corporation in the process. Without hit records, the Grateful Dead achieved elite success, becoming one of the most iconic rock bands of its era and inventing a brand that democratically included their consumers (and literally cocreated a lifestyle for Deadheads).

We're eager to write about the Grateful Dead because we've identified many lessons in what the band has been doing over more than 40 years that can be applied today. These lessons are an important tool for helping to understand the new marketing environment in a language and with examples that are familiar to all. The Grateful Dead is one huge case study in contrarian marketing. Most of the band's many marketing innovations are based on doing the exact opposite of what other bands (and record labels) are doing at the time. Here are just a few examples of what you'll learn in these pages:

1. *Rethink traditional industry assumptions*

    Rather than focus on record albums as a primary revenue source (with touring to support album sales), the Dead created a business model focused on touring.
    Now, entirely new opportunities emerge for those willing to challenge established business models. The Grateful Dead teaches us that business model innovation is frequently more important than product innovation.

2. *Turn your customers into evangelists*

    Unlike nearly every other band, the Grateful Dead not only encouraged concertgoers to record their live shows, they actually established "taper sections" where fans' equipment could be set up for the best sound quality. When nearly every other band said "No," the Grateful Dead created a huge network of people who traded tapes in pre-Web days. The broad exposure led to millions of new fans and sold tickets to the live shows. Today, as many companies experiment with offering valuable content on the Web, the Grateful Dead teaches us that when we free our content, more people hear about our company and eventually do business with us.

3. *Bypass accepted channels and go direct*

   In the early 1970's The Grateful Dead were one of the first bands to create a mailing list where they announced tours to fans first. Later, they established their own ticketing office, providing the most loyal fans with the best seats in the house. The Grateful Dead teaches us that building a community and treating customers with care and respect drives passionate loyalty.

4. *Build a huge, loyal following*

   The Grateful Dead let their audience define the Grateful Dead experience. Concerts were a happening, a destination where all 20,000 or more audience members were actually part of the experience. Making fans an equal partner in a mutual journey, the Grateful Dead teaches us that our community defines who we are. In an era of instant communications on X, blogs, and the like, we learn that companies cannot force a mindset on their customers.

Marketing Lessons from the Grateful Dead will show you how to think and market like the band, which is to think and market differently from your competition. Each chapter presents and analyzes a marketing concept practiced by the Dead and provides a real-world example of a company employing that concept today. We also include a "Rock On" section at the end of each chapter with "to-do" ideas for you.

OUR LONG STRANGE TRIPS

David first heard the band's music just before he started high school. His next-door neighbor, a college student, played Grateful Dead music, loudly, from his bedroom window all summer. The music grew on him and he saw his first live concert on January 17, 1979, in New Haven, Connecticut. He was hooked for life, collecting live concert tapes and seeing the band another 41 times. Brian was in high school when he was indoctrinated into the band by his friend, who blasted the Grateful Dead while they painted houses on Cape Cod during the summer. Brian hitchhiked to his first concert in Saratoga Springs, New York, and that concert sparked a lifelong love—he's seen over 100 shows since.

We first met in 2007 after Brian had read David's book *The New Rules of Marketing & PR* and invited David to the HubSpot offices to talk modern marketing. We both saw the amazing potential of Web marketing and had focused our businesses in the emerging area. When Brian saw a Grateful Dead sticker on David's notebook computer, we also bonded as Deadheads. When you've shared the common experience of having seen dozens of Grateful Dead shows, there is an instant kinship. And, perhaps most importantly, we were both lifelong Grateful Dead fans. Our bond was cemented when, a few weeks later, David had a spare ticket to a sold-out

Introduction to the original edition　　　　　　　　　　　　　　　xxiii

Phil Lesh & Friends show (Lesh is the Grateful Dead's bassist) and he sent it to Brian, who until then was ticketless.

Not only had we both been going to concerts for years, we had both been inspired by the great marketing examples set by The Grateful Dead. In each of David's previous five books, there is a reference to the band, and most speeches he's delivered since 2007 include riffs on how the Grateful Dead culture of "losing control" benefits organizations of all kinds. At HubSpot, the market position that Brian built for his company around the new category of "Inbound Marketing" was significantly influenced by how the Grateful Dead created its own music category (they watched "competitors," but never followed them).

In March 2010 we collaborated on a free webinar called "Marketing Lessons from the Grateful Dead." We quietly announced the virtual gig and were amazed when 1,700 people signed up with almost no promotion. So on April Fools' Day, taking a page out of the Grateful Dead concert playbook, we improvised a discussion on the band's marketing and what companies can learn from it. The feedback from over 300 tweets and a bunch of blog posts was so overwhelmingly positive, we knew we had to do more. This book was born.

PLAYING IN THE BAND

We've organized the book into short, snappy chapters, each focused on one element of the Grateful Dead's marketing. We explain how the band pioneered a technique, provide details, and then give a modern example of an organization using the strategy today. Although we've grouped the chapters into sections, we've written them as stand-alone units that you should feel free to read in any order. (After all, the Grateful Dead hated authority and encouraged independent behavior in fans, so who are we to tell you how to read this book!)

Throughout these pages, you'll be treated to remarkable photographs from Jay Blakesberg, a San Francisco–based photographer whose work has appeared on hundreds of covers and in feature articles for numerous magazines, including *Rolling Stone*, *Guitar World*, and *Guitar Player*. Blakesberg began photographing the Grateful Dead as a high-school student in 1978 and joined the traveling caravan that followed the band in the 1980s. In later years, he worked closely with the band and was given access to create much more intimate and exclusive images.

The amazing original illustrations in the book are by Richard Biffle, an artist whose mystical fantasy pieces inspire many minds. For more than 20 years, Biffle has been working with the Grateful Dead (as well as the individual band members and their spinoff projects), creating the fantastic artwork seen on Dead posters, merchandise, and CD covers.

A note about our use of the band's name: With the 1995 death of founding member and spiritual leader Jerry Garcia, the band's name—the Grateful Dead—was retired when referring to live concerts. While the name continued to be used for the sales of recordings and merchandise, the

Grateful Dead would never play again, and musicians from the band pursued solo careers. From 1998 to 2002, surviving members occasionally re-formed and toured under the name The Other Ones. In 2003, The Other Ones changed their name to The Dead, and then in 2009 a smaller offshoot called Furthur was formed. For simplicity, throughout the book we refer to the Grateful Dead in present tense, choosing not to draw a distinction between touring band names over the past 15 years, and instead treating the Grateful Dead as a band with a continuous 45-year history. The music never stopped.

We've enjoyed working on this book because it combines our personal friendship, our love for the Grateful Dead, and our intense interest in marketing into one focused project.

We hope that our 50 combined years of intense interest in the Grateful Dead together with decades of marketing experience has created a book that's valuable to both Grateful Dead fans and marketers alike.

Preface

WHAT EVERY CEO SHOULD LEARN FROM JERRY GARCIA
BY BRIAN HALLIGAN

There were two leaders I emulated along HubSpot's path from $0 to $25 billion: Steve Jobs and Jerry Garcia. A lot of ink has been spilled about Jobs, but for this CEO, Garcia was just as influential. He had a fundamentally novel approach to pretty much everything, and his ideas were instrumental in how I ran HubSpot in the 15 years since this book was first released. Here are some highlights of what I learned from him in hopes that you can, too.

NOT JUST PASSION, OBSESSION

These days, I spend a lot of my time coaching Sequoia Capital's *startup founders* on their journey to becoming *scale-up* CEOs. As part of that journey, I've gone deep into the "trillion-dollar club CEOs": founder/CEOs of companies that reached a trillion-dollar valuation at some point. All of these folks—Steve Jobs, Bill Gates, Jensen Huang, Jeff Bezos, Larry Page, Mark Zuckerberg, Elon Musk—have one common trait: pure,

all-consuming obsession. They aren't just motivated; they aren't just passionate; they're obsessed with their craft. So was Jerry Garcia.

Garcia played 2,314 concerts with the Grateful Dead over 30 years. It was a grueling set of annual marathons in and of itself. In between these marathons he turned around and played another 1,500 concerts with his side project, the Jerry Garcia Band. He also wrote over 100 of those songs he played with his collaborator, Robert Hunter.

His daughter remembers him spending time with the family watching TV and playing chords on his unplugged guitar constantly; his bandmates recall him noodling on the guitar during almost every meal. He lived and breathed his art. That kind of deep, relentless obsession is what I see in the best CEOs I work with—it's a key indicator of future success.

FIRST-PRINCIPLES THINKING

One thing I tried to do at HubSpot—sometimes successfully, sometimes not—was to always question conventional wisdom. We'd always ask, "If we were designing this from scratch, ignoring precedent, how would we do it?" Garcia lived this mindset.

Where most 1960s bands were cutting 3-minute singles from the studio, the Dead were jamming 30-minute soliloquies on the stage several nights a week.

Where their peers all fit neatly into the rock genre, the Dead created their own: the jam band.

Where album sales were the revenue engine du jour, the Dead made their living on live shows.

Where everyone was outsourcing their ticket sales to middle operators (i.e., Ticketmaster), the Dead cut out the middle person, built their own ticketing operation, and put their fans' experience first.

Where radio placements were the industry's marketing vehicle, the Dead created a freemium, viral distribution model letting their fans trade their live shows via cassette tapes.

This first-principles approach made their business—and their art—profoundly different.

I think CEOs should pick their battles where they rethink versus follow, but in my humble opinion, there needs to be a whole lot more rethinking going on.

SPIKEY (NOT WELL-ROUNDED) TALENT

When scaling a company, it's a huge temptation to hire "well-rounded" executive talent. The bigger your company gets, the more people you include in the interview process, the more likely you are to hire the candidate with the least weaknesses as opposed to the candidate with a combination of spikey strengths and spikey weaknesses. I'll give you an example. Let's say a company has 8 internal folks interview candidate A and candidate B. For candidate A, half of them are 4/10 and half are 10/10. For candidate B, all of them are 7/10s. Almost inevitably, the scaling company goes with candidate B, the one with the "least weaknesses." More often than not, that company is looking for a replacement for candidate B 18 months later.

Okay, so what about Garcia? When he was forming the band, he went with all As. The band was formed a few years after the Beatles and the Rolling Stones in the first phases of the rock'n'roll era. Garcia himself was a bluegrass banjo player. When selecting bandmates, he steered clear of folks like himself. His bass player, Phil Lesh, was a classically trained jazz trumpet player whom Garcia convinced to learn the bass. His keyboard player, Ron "Pigpen" McKernan, was a bluesman. One of his drummers (they had two!) was a drum majorette in a marching band.

Jerry built a spikey team and stayed away from hiring folks in his own image. It's the spikes—not the well-roundedness—that drive breakthroughs in the companies I work with.

TEAMWORK ACTUALLY DOES MAKE THE DREAM WORK

This spikey set of musicians had to work together in a way that no other band of that era had ever done before. They played similar songs as the Beatles and the Rolling Stones; in fact, they often covered those bands' songs, but they played them in a novel way. The Beatles and the Rolling Stones played structured 3-minute songs. The Grateful Dead played unstructured 30-minute masterpieces. They played rock'n'roll music more like a jazz band. In fact, they never played the same set list twice and they never played the same song the same way.

This type of collaboration involved a level of trust and teamwork that other bands didn't require. Jerry was heavily featured in these collaborations, but it involved brilliant interplay with each player in the band. Jerry described his role this way: "I'm not the best at anything. I'm not a great musician, a great songwriter. I just have this ability to blend in with whatever is going on."

LOW-KEY LEADER

The stars of his era were flashy and attention seeking, think Mick Jagger strutting around stage, Robert Plant's outfits and long mane, Jim Morrison with his shirt off on stage, and so on. Garcia presented himself as a humble musician. Quietly coming on stage with the same simple jeans and black t-shirt thousands of times.

A lot of CEOs have a sort of false modesty that is relatively easy to see through and is kind of cringeworthy. Garcia's modesty was real. He was shy and didn't like the spotlight and his persona to match what was actually going on inside him.

I think this is the way to go for CEOs. The ride for me at HubSpot was always two steps forward, one step back, two steps forward, one step back. The job truly humbled me. I see some early-stage CEOs strutting like Jagger. When the one step back happens, that won't age well.

SUCCESSION SUPERHERO

The Grateful Dead dealt with three deaths of their keyboard players over their 30 years! Each time, they did a masterful

job of recruiting a new keyboard player who added something new and special to the band.

After Jerry's death in 1995, the band seemed finished … until nearly 20 years later, a young guitarist—John Mayer, a pop icon—was recruited to form Dead & Company. To many, including me, this seemed sacrilegious. But when you listened, you heard someone honoring the tradition while adding his own voice.

It's a perfect analogy for companies navigating succession. If you find someone who brings their own style while honoring the past, renewal is not only possible but it also can be powerful. Microsoft's transformation under Satya Nadella after going sideways with Steve Ballmer is a perfect example of this.

PRINCE OF PALO ALTO

The Grateful Dead were founded in Palo Alto and had their first "real" concert at Stanford University in the middle of the 1960s. This was a place and time in history of tremendous creativity that grew out of the acid test parties, the beatnik poets, and the Summer of Love. The Grateful Dead were the soundtrack of that era and were born of this primordial soup.

I don't think it is a coincidence that this free-wheeling, free-thinking, free-loving place was also the home of what was later termed Silicon Valley. I see the ethos of the Grateful

Dead and this era running through the veins of entrepreneurs from Steve Jobs to Sam Altman.

If I were founding a new company, I'd be awfully tempted to start it down the street from where Jerry and friends got started. It was fertile soil 60 years ago and still is today.

CONTINUING JOURNEY WITH JERRY

The Grateful Dead, and particularly Jerry Garcia, profoundly influenced me—not just in designing HubSpot but also in understanding how to lead the team and the community.

This book is filled with stories, lessons, and strategies from their journey—a journey that challenged the norms and reshaped what a successful enterprise can be. I hope it sparks your imagination and guides you to lead in your own way—just as Jerry did.

BOBBY WEIR AND THE MUSIC THAT WILL NEVER STOP
by DAVID MEERMAN SCOTT

It's October 2022 and I'm experiencing Grateful Dead music like I never have before. Bobby Weir & Wolf Bros featuring The Wolfpack are playing the Kennedy Center in a unique collaboration with the National Symphony Orchestra. With the addition of nearly 100 classical musicians dialed into orchestration by Stanford professor Dr. Giancarlo Aquilanti, Grateful Dead fan favorites like" Jack Straw," "Shakedown Street," "Playing in the Band," and "Touch of Gray" have never sounded like this. Of the over 1,000 live music shows I've seen since I was 15 years old, hundreds of bands of various genres, this was a top 10 highlight. Here was Bobby fronting the music I love, performed in a new and wonderful way, utterly different than my first Grateful Dead show in New Haven on January 17, 1979.

I'm imagining Jerry looking down with a huge smile on his face as he watches Bobby push the music of the Grateful Dead forward yet again. Indeed, in the 30 years since Jerry's passing, I'd argue the Grateful Dead has become more popular and culturally significant than during the Jerry years.

They are most certainly bigger and better than in 2010 when the first edition of this book appeared.

PLAYING IN THE BRAND

Bobby's focus over three decades—launching new bands, embracing younger collaborators, pushing technology forward, championing charitable causes, and overseeing projects that preserve the Dead's history—ensures the band's legacy thrives and reaches younger generations.

When Jerry passed in August 1995, the surviving members and fans alike thought the journey was over. "When Jerry left, that was the end of the Grateful Dead. Period," drummer Bill Kreutzmann said. Yet Bobby quickly found ways to continue playing the music. In the decades since, he has anchored numerous offshoots, including RatDog, The Other Ones, The Dead, Furthur, Bob Weir & Wolf Bros, and Dead & Company. With these collaborations Bobby ensured the music never stopped.

Bringing John Mayer into the Grateful Dead fold to form Dead & Company was certainly controversial. I spoke with many people who couldn't wrap their heads around the idea of a 30-something pop star joining three of the surviving members of the Grateful Dead —Bobby Weir, Mickey Hart, and Bill Kreutzmann—together with Oteil Burbridge and Jeff Chimenti. Yet, the combination proved infectious with older enthusiasts like me and brought many new fans into the scene.

The original Grateful Dead were one of the highest-grossing music acts of the early 1990s, selling over nine million tickets and grossing about $227 million in that decade. The Dead & Company final tour in summer 2023 alone drew about 850,000 fans across 28 shows, grossing over $100 million. So, yeah, they are a major concert draw by every measure.

In 2024, at age 77, Bobby led Dead & Company into yet another musical collaboration, a residency at the newly opened Sphere in Las Vegas. With immersive multimedia shows at the world's most sophisticated venue, longtime fans and newbies alike were mesmerized at the Sphere by the crystal-clear sound and the trippy graphics on the world's largest and highest-resolution LED screen. I went to six shows at Sphere that first year, enjoying the newest Dead spectacle. Clips of Dead & Company at Sphere, with psychedelic visuals and all-out jams, quickly lit up TikTok and Instagram. Suddenly a band whose popularity peaked when Mark Zuckerberg was barely out of diapers was trending on social media more than 30 years later.

TOUCH OF LEGACY

In the years since we wrote the first edition of this book, Bobby has brought talented young musicians into the Grateful Dead fold. He's been a guest on stages such as that of Billy Strings and The National, invited sit-ins at his shows from the likes of Tyler Childers and Daniel Donato, and curated the Playing in the Sand and Dead Ahead festivals in Mexico, which included artists and acts like Larkin Poe, Tedeschi Trucks, Rick Mitarotonda, Margo Price, Sturgill Simpson, Sierra Hull, and others. And, of course, there's John Mayer.

These frequent collaborations help to introduce the music of the Grateful Dead to the fans of these artists and serve as a spark for younger players to keep the music alive for decades to come.

Bobby has also built a community through his frequent philanthropic endeavors. He's committed to social and environmental causes in the past several decades, reinforcing the Dead's legacy is about kindness and unity as much as music. After Garcia's death, the Rex Foundation, the Dead's charitable arm, stayed active with Bobby frequently lending his time and name to benefit events.

He has worked with Reverb, which promotes eco-friendly touring, to make sure Dead-related tours have a positive impact. Starting in 2015, Dead & Company institutionalized giving back with Participation Row at their shows—a village of booths where nonprofits engage with fans, encouraging concertgoers to take action on causes from sustainability to social action. During their final 2023 tour alone, Deadheads contributed over $2 million via Participation Row charities. And Bobby is on the board of HeadCount, a nonprofit that has registered over a million people to vote at concerts and music festivals.

RIPPLE THROUGH TIME

Since the first edition of this book released, we lost Grateful Dead bassist Phil Lesh. And we lost our friend Bill Walton, who wrote the fabulous Foreword to this book.

Bobby was just 17 years old when he joined what would become the Grateful Dead. Now, some 60 years later, he has evolved into one of rock's premier elder statesmen. He's become a living emblem of the Dead's longevity and countercultural legacy. Someday, when there are no longer any original members of the Grateful Dead able to perform, this music will live on because of Bobby's efforts.

PART ONE
THE BAND

CHAPTER 1
Create a Unique Business Model

Before the Web, bands promoted their new albums by scheduling tours across the United States and around the world. Fans paid huge bucks to attend sold-out shows, where they were treated to pyrotechnics, light shows, and, of course, the music. Concerts were the same every night and included the bands' "best of" songs, with cuts from the new album mixed throughout the set. The goal of these concert tours was to sell as many records as possible to ensure that an album went gold or platinum.

Fans bought albums at their local record store, where they would find the list of top albums for that week taped to the wall next to the cash register. For an album to go to gold in 1975, a band had to sell 500,000 records and hit $1 million in sales. To be awarded the coveted platinum certification, bands had to sell one million albums and hit the $2 million sales mark.

Doing concert tours to promote these moneymaking albums was the fundamental business model for bands, the record labels, and sundry hangers-on. The Grateful Dead turned this business model on its ear: rather than focusing on selling albums, like other bands, they focused on generating revenue from live concerts, and in doing so created a fan "experience" that was unlike any other.

Because the concert tours themselves were the main source of revenue, the Grateful Dead ran their concerts in a very different way from other bands. For example, each show had a unique set of songs, and each song was played in a unique way, giving fans a strong incentive to see the show for several nights in a row (or weeks, months, or years), because every night you were treated to a different musical experience. This is the exact opposite approach to that taken by other bands.

Since the concert tour was at the heart of their business model, the Grateful Dead didn't tour periodically to promote an album; with few exceptions, they were permanently on tour. The Grateful Dead invested heavily in their light show and sound systems, both of which were the best in the industry, and in doing so made the musical experience much more powerful for their fans.

Due to these factors and others, the Grateful Dead developed a following of people who would see show after show. These followers became part of the concert experience, especially as you waded through them in the parking lot, where you were exposed to tasty foods such as veggie burritos, all sorts of exotic drugs, unique clothing, and all the other crazy stuff that went along with a Dead tour.

By changing that one fundamental assumption in a typical band's business model, the Grateful Dead created a cascading effect of benefits for themselves and their fans.

 > THE GRATEFUL DEAD CREATED A BUSINESS MODEL THAT WAS THE EXACT OPPOSITE OF EVERY OTHER BAND'S AT THE TIME.

Imagine for a moment if the Grateful Dead had put themselves in the care of a manager who was focused on selling records and increasing the profits of a record company. If they had conformed to "industry best practices," the Grateful Dead might be one of the thousands of bands on the dead heap of music history. The concert-as-business-model worked, and the Dead created a passionate fan base that became an underground cult that catapulted the Grateful Dead into the rock-and-roll stratosphere: the fan base grew from thousands to hundreds of thousands to millions, with the Grateful Dead selling out shows year after year.

MARKETING LESSON FROM THE GRATEFUL DEAD
Create a Unique Business Model

It's much easier to follow what other companies are doing and mimic their business model than it is to innovate. Don't do it! Watch your competition, but avoid the temptation to follow them with every fiber of your soul.

Today's big winners typically won because of unique business model assumptions, rather than some new technology or complicated product improvements. A few common examples include Netflix (versus Blockbuster), Zipcar (versus Hertz), eBay (versus yard sale), Google AdWords (versus Yahoo), iPod and iTunes (versus MP3s and downloading), Southwest Airlines (versus driving long-distance), and Walmart (versus the local store). Like the Grateful Dead, these companies turned the core assumption of how their industry works on its head to create an unlevel playing field for themselves. Their rejection of core assumptions in their industry allowed them to really stand out from their competition and create a cascade of benefits for their customers.

> THE GRATEFUL DEAD TEACHES US THAT BUSINESS MODEL INNOVATION IS JUST AS IMPORTANT, IF NOT MORE SO, THAN PRODUCT INNOVATION.

RUE LA LA CREATES ONLINE BUYING DESTINATION FOR LUXURY GOODS

An exclusive, invitation-only online destination, Rue La La is a web site where members can purchase high-end fashion goods at discounted prices. What's different about Rue La La from a T. J. Maxx or other discount retailers is its business model. Rather than offer last year's items that didn't sell in the stores at heavily discounted prices, Rue La La developed partnerships with designers and, by working closely with them, offers current merchandise and one-of-a-kind items at discounted prices—items that can only be purchased during limited time periods.

Here's how it works: Each day, Rue La La features a designer boutique, say Villeroy & Boch or St. John, that opens at 11:00 A.M. Eastern and remains open for 48 hours or until merchandise sells out, with a blinking clock counting down the time. Because merchandise can sell out in a matter of minutes, members often set calendar reminders so that they can be at their computers a few minutes before 11:00 A.M. The company sends out e-mail reminders a few days in advance that let people know which designers will be featured on the site.

Since its inception in April 2008, Rue La La has built a passionate fan base of 1.6 million members using viral methods. To become a member, you must receive an invitation from another member. Once a member extends an invitation, he or she receives a $10 credit when each friend places their first order, with no limit placed on the number of credits one can receive. Credits can then be used against any boutique purchase.

You would think that the limited availability of fashion items would frustrate people and turn them away. Instead, the opposite is true: Limited availability of items reduces over exposure of brand partners and their merchandise, as well as customer fatigue caused by seeing the same brand or fashion items over and over again. It also creates a sense of urgency—if shoppers don't buy something immediately, they'll lose out and will kick themselves for days afterward for missing a good deal. This is different from the typical shopping experience in which, if you're not sure about an item, you can go home and "think about it," which usually means a no-sale for the retailer as your ardor cools and you realize you don't really "need" the item.

Rue La La helps people make fast purchases with its "Quick! Buy It" feature: a member enters her credit card number and billing/shipping information on the account settings page, and when shopping can click the "Quick! Buy It" button, eliminating the number of clicks needed for hot purchases. Members can even shop via smart phone—making it easy to purchase items while on the run. If a member has a problem with any purchase, she or he can Tweet Rue La La's Concierge, who responds immediately.

Instead of competing with retail discounters or high-end department stores, Rue La La has created an innovative business model that targets a distinctive demographic. With passionate fans around the world, the company grew from around $25 million in sales in 2008 to $28 million in the third quarter alone for 2009. Their business model "paid off" as the company was purchased by GSI Commerce, Inc., in early 2010 for $350 million.

ROCK ON

Create your own landscape

Products that are highly differentiated can still succeed today, but it's much harder to win if your business model is the same as your competitors'. Your job is to do research about your industry in order to build a killer business model. You want to break free from the competitive landscape and create a cascade of unique benefits for your customers.

ACTION: Creating a unique business model is very difficult and no free lunch exists on how to do it. Rather than tell you how to create a unique business model in your industry, we thought we would give you some hard questions to ask yourself that will get your juices flowing about how to create one:

What are you three times better at than your competitors? What are you three times worse at than your competitors? If the answer is "nothing" to both, you are not unique enough to really break out. And no, you can't be better than your competition in all dimensions—you need to rethink the dimensions.

What new technology is emerging that might enable you to upset your industry's apple cart? Could the Web be a new distribution channel? Could an iPad application catapult you past the competition? Could you use Artificial Intelligence to dramatically lower costs or deliver new value?

Are there societal changes happening that you might take advantage of in your industry, such as empty nesters moving back into cities, more people working from home, a shift to outsourcing to rural America rather than overseas, or increased interest in low-carbon-footprint lifestyles for companies and families, and so on?

Do you have someone who's really smart from outside your industry whom you can ask to help you with this? The problem with creating a unique business model in an industry you grew up in is that you naturally get bogged down in the same industry assumptions that you're trying to break.

CHAPTER 2
Choose Memorable Brand (and Band) Names

The Grateful Dead.

If you stop to think about it, the name is sorta weird. Even a little scary.

But, boy, is it memorable.

Originally calling themselves the Warlocks when they formed a band in 1965, the musicians realized they needed to come up with a new name a year later when they found out that there was another band by the same name that had recorded a single. The guys debated names, coming up with ideas such as "Mythical Ethical Icicle Tricycle" (Garcia) and "His Own Sweet Advocates" (Weir). When they were unable to find a name they agreed on, they gathered at Phil Lesh's house around a copy of *Bartlett's Quotations*, read out a thousand possible names, but couldn't agree on anything. Then Jerry Garcia opened a copy of *Funk and Wagnall's New Practical Standard Dictionary* (1956 edition) and randomly pointed to a page. There, staring back at him, was *grateful dead*. Several members immediately fell in love with the name and wanted to use it. Others were a bit wary. But all agreed it was memorable, so they decided to use it.

> LOVE IT, HATE IT, OR DON'T UNDERSTAND IT—WHATEVER YOU MAY THINK OF IT, THE GRATEFUL DEAD IS A NAME THAT YOU REMEMBER.

The dictionary defines the term as a type of ballad involving a hero who helps a corpse who is being refused a proper burial, a theme found in many cultures. For the Grateful Dead, the strange cosmic quality the name evokes—a world beyond consciousness—was perfect. This, of course, played into what the band was doing on stage. That some in the audience might be experimenting with mind-altering substances while listening to a band called the Grateful Dead made the name choice interesting on another level.

Fast-forward to four decades later and the name seems ideal. The choice of name worked to help advance the Grateful Dead to its widely recognized status as the most iconic band in history. And the sort of inside-joke quality—a name that your parents likely hated and your less-cool schoolmates or coworkers scoffed at—contributed to the community aspect of those in the know. A badge of honor was bestowed upon those who were independent enough to enjoy a band with such an odd name.

Marketing Lesson from the Grateful Dead
Choose Memorable Brand Names

A name—like the Grateful Dead—is an asset to an organization. When you select an uncommon name (and one appropriate to your company image and target market) it's unlikely that consumers will confuse your product with something similar. They will remember you. And in today's world of online communications and of search engines, unique names for your company, products, and services allow you to own the search engine results for your brands.

> The Grateful Dead teaches us that a memorable name can bring success.

Most companies don't focus enough attention on choosing a memorable name or on the importance of Google, other search engines, and AI chatbots when selecting those names. Typically people closest to the product development effort are the ones proposing the candidate names. This usually leads to overly technical names focused on what a product does (something like "MP3 Deluxe Pocket Player" rather than a memorable name that appeals to customers, like "iPod").

At most companies, candidate names are vetted by the legal department for copyright and trademark issues that would disqualify use, but few bother to do a Google search on the potential new name. If your company's web site is not on the first page of the Google results with searches for your product name, that should disqualify it as an option.

HUBSPOT AND DAVID MEERMAN SCOTT

Allow us to share our own personal stories.

When Brian and HubSpot cofounder Dharmesh Shah founded the company in 2006, they needed a memorable name. They thought up HubSpot when trying to describe how your web site should be turned from a billboard in the desert into a living breathing "hub" for your marketplace. That, combined with the double entendre for Boston (nicknamed The Hub [of the Universe]), which is much like the company name "Cisco" (for San Francisco), made it a good choice. People in the market liked the name because the information that they provided on their site and blog served to fill the name with meaning (as in a "hub" of information).

Unlike most technology companies, HubSpot does not focus on product brand names. It's just HubSpot. So there isn't confusion in the market about what people are buying. The name is memorable.

Like Brian's method in researching the name HubSpot, David also paid very close attention to choosing a brand name. He has used his middle name—Meerman—in his professional endeavors since 2001. Some of David's family originated from Dordrecht in the Netherlands, and Meerman is the middle name of firstborn sons going back generations. David chose to use Meerman to differentiate himself from the hordes of other "David Scotts" out there, many of whom have racked up their own accomplishments. One David Scott walked on the moon as commander of Apollo 15. Another David Scott is a six-time Iron Man Triathlon Champion. And yet another David Scott was a member of the U.S. House of Representatives from Georgia's 13th district. Certainly David is in good company, but to be memorable, for clarity, and to be found in search engines, he chose to become unique among his fellow David Scotts.

The next time you need to name a company, product, book, album, or service, you need to make certain that you can own the search results for your name. Although Brian was able to get the domain name HubSpot.com and David secured DavidMeermanScott.com, the ability to get the domain name for your product or service is less important than the ability for you to come up at the top of the first page of the search engine results.

ROCK ON

Find your memorable name

Naming is tough. But it is a very important element of marketing. Most organizations don't spend enough time on this important activity.

ACTION: Here are some things to keep in mind and a few tricks you might try as you think of a name:

- Avoid common names and names that are already used as a title of a popular movie or book. You will want to have a name that shows up as the top listing for search results in the search engines and social media sites.

- Use search engines before finalizing a name. You don't want to fall in love with a name that doesn't yield the top search results.

- Find inspiration in unlikely places. Why not go to one of the online booksellers (such as Amazon.com, BN.com, or Borders.com) and search the name of the category of product you are trying to name. You'll see a list of book titles and subtitles that may spark an idea.

- Many people choose made-up words as a name. This is great because you can own the search results. But try not to choose one that is too esoteric or difficult to pronounce if you go this route.

- You might take two words that are very different and put them together as one word, like SurveyMonkey, an intriguing company name.

- Try an alternative spelling for a word. "Google" is derived from the word "googol," a number that is 10 to the power of 100 (the numeral one followed by 100 zeros). "Flickr" is "flicker" with the "e" removed.

- In her excellent book *POP!*, Sam Horn talks about what she calls "alphabetizing" common words to come up with a name. We like this technique. Take a product you want to name, for example, yogurt in a squeeze tube. Then go through every letter in the alphabet and substitute it for the "y" in yogurt, and presto: "GoGurt" is born.

- Take a common name and change it slightly to create a new word. For example, the name of the social networking site FledgeWing is derived from the word "fledgling."

Chapter 3
Build a Diverse Team

Some argue that the Grateful Dead were not the best musicians, but their deeply diverse backgrounds made for a powerful combination that created a sound unlike any other.

Jerry Garcia, the Grateful Dead's lead guitarist, also played bluegrass banjo, an influence that added to the Dead's category-defying sound. In fact, Garcia participated in numerous bluegrass side projects throughout his lifetime including his excellent band "Old and In the Way." You can hear this influence in Grateful Dead cuts such as "Ripple" and "Friend of the Devil."

Bassist Phil Lesh, on the other hand, began his career as a classical jazz musician who played trumpet; he learned bass guitar "on the job" after joining the Grateful Dead early on. Because he didn't know how to play bass, he didn't bring preconceived notions to the job. His willingness to experiment and learn resulted in his playing a significant role in defining the Grateful Dead's distinctive sound—and ultimately becoming one of music's most influential bass players.

Ron "Pigpen" McKernan, the Grateful Dead's first keyboard player, the son of an R&B disc jockey, was a blues harmonica player and also a keyboardist before he joined the band.

His background added yet another twist to the Grateful Dead's unique sound.

> THE GRATEFUL DEAD COMBINED DIVERSE SKILLS FOR A SYNERGISTIC 1 + 1 = 3 SOUND THAT HAD NEVER BEEN HEARD BEFORE.

When bands form, they're typically made up of people with similar musical backgrounds. And if a member dies or leaves the group, the band will hold auditions to ensure that the replacement can easily fit in with the band's sound.

The Grateful Dead, on the other hand, seemed to attract musicians with widely diverse backgrounds. Keith Godchaux joined the band after his wife grabbed Garcia at a show to say her husband would make a perfect keyboardist for the band (McKernan having stepped down due to ill health); although Godchaux had not studied the Grateful Dead or their music and was primarily an acoustic piano player, he tried out—and was immediately signed on.

In addition to having musicians with diverse backgrounds, the Grateful Dead often had musicians with very little experience and even less formal education. Guitarist and singer Bob Weir was a high school student when he founded the Grateful Dead with Jerry Garcia. The mix of unique backgrounds unencumbered by conventional wisdom proved to be a powerful combination.

MARKETING LESSON FROM THE GRATEFUL DEAD
Build a Diverse Team

In today's world things are changing fast, so, like the Grateful Dead, you need a marketing team comprised of individuals with diverse, unique talents that didn't necessarily originate in a marketing department, PR firm, or ad agency. You need people who are "digital citizens" (think bluegrass background) hardwired for the Web. In other words, you want people who instinctively understand how the Web works or at least know the right questions to ask.

To build a great marketing team, you need highly analytical types (think jazz background) who speak the language of AI as well as their native tongue. In a perfect world, you would have folks on your team with deep reach (think blues background) into the marketplace. Traditionally, people with "reach" had Rolodexes stuffed with hundreds of industry contacts. Now you need people whose reach includes thousands in the blogosphere and social mediasphere. Finally, you need people who are facile with creating content (think R&B background): white papers, blogs, videos, e-books, webinars, and podcasts. You won't find all of these traits in one person, so you should build a team of people who hold these various skills.

When hiring the individuals with these skills, you'll want to consider people who don't come from traditional marketing, advertising, or PR backgrounds and are completely unencumbered by the "best practices" developed during an era when your marketplace watched ads, answered cold calls, opened e-mail blasts, and attended trade shows. For example, there are lots of out-of-work journalists out there who would make

great content creators. A freshly minted MBA who understands pivot tables might make a great analytical hire. Someone with a TikTok channel in your support department might have great "reach" for you. A blogger in your industry who is living in her parent's basement because she cannot figure out how to monetize her content might make a perfect content creator.

If you look at most marketing job descriptions today, you'll see that most companies are still mired in old ways, even though the behaviors of their target market have totally changed: "Write and maintain print and online sales collateral, including web site," "Support PR activities," and so forth. Use this fact to your advantage and jump ahead of your marketplace to build a diverse team with unique talents that can help you match the way you market to the way your marketplace shops and buys! What you don't want to do in today's world is to hire a lot of marketing generalists with heavily overlapping skill sets in "project management."

 THE GRATEFUL DEAD TEACHES US TO FIND TALENTED PEOPLE OUTSIDE OF OUR INDUSTRY AND COMFORT ZONES.

DIGITAL DIVA JULIA ROY BRINGS SOCIAL SKILLS TO COACH

It used to be that to find out what was new and hot in the world of fashion, you had to buy glossy, richly illustrated magazines stuffed full of ads or tune in to a TV show highlighting the lives of the rich and famous. Luxury brands carefully monitored their brands as overexposure opened them to the masses—diluting their image of exclusivity. For this reason luxury brands have been hesitant to embrace social media. The Web is for the masses, the thinking goes, and therefore social media opens the brand to everyone.

Yet like most people these days, affluent shoppers have moved online for the sake of convenience, and luxury brands need to keep up. One way to do that is by hiring someone like Julia Roy—which is what luxury handbag maker Coach did when the company brought her on board in 2009. Roy is from completely outside the fashion industry, but she's a digital citizen, she's analytical and has broad reach, and she's a natural-born content creator.

Roy doesn't have a traditional corporate marketing or PR background or an MBA. After completing her degree in International Relations, Public Policy, and Political Science at Simmons College in Boston, Massachusetts, Roy realized that she didn't want a career in political science and fell into working on a fundraising campaign called "Making Change for Katrina," where she developed a web site and blog—and made a life-changing discovery: The two-week old "Making Change" blog ranked higher in the search engines than the more established web site did. Roy asked, "How could this poorly designed and makeshift blog be considered by Google to have more 'authority' than the web site?!" She set out to find out why.

So began her odyssey into social media and emerging digital communities. Along the way, she amassed a following through her own personal branding strategies, including over 40,000 X followers and 3,000 Facebook fans.

And that job at Coach? Roy became the Senior Manager of New Media of the company's nascent Global Web and Digital Media department and is helping the luxury retailer incorporate social media tactics. In this case, Coach did the exact right thing by bringing in someone from completely outside their industry, who was unencumbered by an older set of assumptions and who had a skill-set that was likely completely different from their existing marketing staff.

ROCK ON

Rethink your marketing department

Does your marketing team look like everyone else's? Is your marketing organization set up the same way as that of your last company? Is your marketing organization full of "generalist project manager" types who have heavily overlapping skill-sets? If so, it's time for a change in organization, some new skills development, and new blood (i.e., Julia Roy–style).

ACTION: Organize your marketing team in this way: You want someone responsible for "getting found" (filling the top of your funnel), someone responsible for "converting" the folks who are getting pulled in, and someone responsible for "analyzing" the numbers and helping you make better decisions.

Try to diversify the skill-set in your marketing department and fill in the gaps by hiring or training folks to be digital citizens ("convert team"), who understand AI ("analyze team"), have deep market reach ("get found team") and/or are natural-born content creators ("get found team").

Look outside your marketing department (inside your company) and look outside the marketing industry (outside your company) to fill in talent gaps.

CHAPTER 4
Be Yourself

In an era when many bands were known for their outrageous costumes and slick onstage personas, the Grateful Dead stood out. Shunning the glitter suits and makeup of glam rockers and the polished Mod look of the British bands, Grateful Dead members were simply themselves—dope-smoking, music-loving, San Francisco hippies.

Band members appeared on stage looking a lot like their fans: donning long hair, scruffy beards, and Birkenstocks, their look didn't change much over the years. By the time Phil Lesh was in his forties, he looked less like an aging rocker and more like someone's mild-mannered next-door neighbor as he played bass guitar in his jeans and T-shirt. In fact, he looked a lot like many of the aging Deadheads in the audience.

Unlike most live concerts, which were highly orchestrated, repeatable events, the Grateful Dead's concerts were completely unscripted, which meant that band members often made mistakes. Sometimes they'd start a song, weren't able to get into it, and would just stop playing it. When they made mistakes musically, they simply shrugged it off and moved on. Their fans understood and accepted this as part of the Grateful Dead experience. After all, they were human, too.

 **THE GRATEFUL DEAD'S AUTHENTICITY ENDEARED THEM TO THEIR FANS.**

While the Grateful Dead did have PR people and managers, the band still managed to keep a certain intimacy between themselves and their fans. Instead of buying ads to create interest in their music or issuing "corporate speak" mailings, the Grateful Dead sent out newsletters that described their "journey," such as this introspective paragraph from a Spring 1972 issue:

> You probably have been wondering what it's all about . . . just as much as we have at times. We originally had hopes of establishing some sort of communication system between all of you out there. However, our own lack of money has prevented us from doing what we originally intended.

MARKETING LESSON FROM THE GRATEFUL DEAD
Be Yourself

Businesses today can learn from the Grateful Dead about being authentic. Customers, partners, and employees appreciate authentic transparency more than ever as a younger generation grows up, becomes consumers, and enters the workforce with different ideas around these topics.

The marketplace is incredibly forgiving of mistakes—especially if a company owns up to a mistake immediately, explains how or why the mistake happened, and how the company is fixing it. People are far less forgiving when mistakes are covered up—as we saw when Toyota attempted to cover up its sticking accelerator problem. Lack of transparency is especially problematic for younger generations who have grown up posting their life events on Facebook. For these people, "privacy" and "transparency" have much different meanings than they do for someone who didn't grow up in the digital age.

> **THE GRATEFUL DEAD TEACHES US THAT MISTAKES ARE QUICKLY FORGIVEN IF YOU'RE TRANSPARENT.**

Rather than blocking employees from TikTok and Instagram, encourage them to use these tools. Set loose guidelines for what they can post about and then let them go for it. Your trust in them will be rewarded in spades as these employees will build their own followings, who will eventually buy your products. If they or you make a mistake, it's okay. Own up to it rather than hiding it—or worse yet, ignoring it. The benefits of the upside far outweigh the potential downside.

Stop hiding your personality behind carefully scripted announcements, press releases, and events. Be yourself, and encourage your CEO and employees to be themselves. If you've got a quirky company culture, your marketplace might prefer that to the corporate façade you're putting on. Eliminate the "corporate-ese" language from press releases and your web site, and show more of who you are and what your company stands for.

SALESFORCE.COM OWNS UP TO MISTAKES AND BUILDS TRUST IN THE PROCESS

In its early days, Salesforce.com, a web-based CRM company, experienced a number of outages—including a 2005 service outage that lasted over three hours. These outages didn't bode well because at the time web-based applications were still moving into the mainstream and the people who were considering them were worried that keeping their most important data "in the cloud" would mean they couldn't access it should the application "go down" for hours at a time.

After the 2005 outage, Salesforce.com's rivals were quick to seize the opportunity to flood the Web and journalists' inboxes with negative Salesforce.com publicity. Salesforce.com took a lot of heat—from both the press and its customers. Rather than ignore the outage, or blame the third-party vendor who managed the data cluster, Salesforce.com acknowledged their mistake and started a new web site—Trust.Salesforce.com—which showed system status 24 hours a day, seven days a week. In fact, the first sentence on the Trust site reads "Security begins with trust. And trust begins with transparency." Anyone can access real-time information about Salesforce.com's system performance and uptime.

By developing the Trust site, Salesforce.com made themselves—and the mistake they made—accessible to the world and, in doing so, earned tremendous trust from their customers. This level of transparency endeared them to corporate IT people, who were among the decision-makers for their offering. This extreme transparency move was one important decision, among many, that helped Salesforce.com become worth over $10 billion within 10 years of its founding.

ROCK ON
Set your employees free

So much in the modern marketing world is consistent with what our parents taught us as kids. Our parents taught us to be ourselves, to be honest, to apologize for our mistakes, and to earn people's trust.

ACTION: Encourage employees to contribute to your company blog or talk about your company on social networks. Let them know you trust them to do the right thing—this trust will be rewarded. To help everyone take advantage of your new policy regarding social media, announce a Lunch-and-Learn about best practices, proper use, and so forth. If you don't have the expertise, go online and search for webinars on the topic and show these at your Lunch-and-Learns.

Speak like a human in your releases, not like a press release robot. Your marketplace's mother tongue is human—it speaks press release robot as a second language.

If you make a mistake, own up to it—don't try to hide it.

CHAPTER 5
Experiment, Experiment, Experiment

The Grateful Dead played over 2,300 concerts and each one was completely unique due to their improvisational style. Jerry Garcia talked about how in every Grateful Dead concert, about 80 percent of the music was improvisation, and 20 percent was more like the standard, repeatable songs, similar to what other bands played at their concerts.

This improvisation wasn't new—jazz musicians had been doing it for years (and greatly influenced the Grateful Dead's style). In jazz performances, a member of the group begins a riff and runs with it, then another member picks it up and builds on it, and so forth. The improvisational elements are sequential with only one musician riffing at a time.

The Grateful Dead, however, improvised individually and as a group—at the same time. Musically, this simultaneous improvisation was profound as it required band members to listen carefully to what each of the other members were doing musically and build on it—while simultaneously carrying on their own improvisational riffs.

> **THE GRATEFUL DEAD EXPERIMENTED WITH MUSICAL FORMS AND GENRES—BOTH AS A GROUP AND INDIVIDUALLY—CREATING UNIQUE MUSICAL EXPERIENCES.**

Truly passionate about experimentation, individual band members constantly worked with different instruments. Garcia, for example, played the electric guitar, bluegrass banjo, pedal steel guitar, and mandolin, while McKernan played keyboard instruments, harmonica, and different percussion instruments. Hart and his partner in drums, fellow Rythym Devil Kreutzmann, experimented with various materials and instruments. During each concert's drums duet, you might hear sounds from metal pipes or garbage cans as well as esoteric instruments like the African talking drum, one of the oldest instruments in the world, used by West African griots.

Because they did so much experimentation/improvisation and because each show was unique, they made a lot more mistakes than most other bands. As Jerry Garcia once said, "You go diving for pearls every night but sometimes you end up with clams." If you attended four or five shows, one or two of them might be a real dud in terms of performance. It wasn't unusual to see a poor show one night followed up by a great show the next night.

The Grateful Dead were their own toughest critic and knew when they laid an egg at a show. Despite the occassional poor performance, they didn't become conservative and stop experimenting. They continued to push the edge and learn from the mistakes they made in the process.

MARKETING LESSON FROM THE GRATEFUL DEAD
Experiment, Experiment, Experiment

Due to the sweeping changes taking place with AI and social media, CEOs and small business owners alike tend to keep a tight rein on marketers, who, out of fear for their jobs, may become overly conservative, overthink decisions, or not take enough risks.

Like the Grateful Dead, marketers today need to experiment in their craft in order to make big breakthroughs. Instead of seeing failure as something to be avoided, CEOs and management teams need to free their marketers to experiment, quickly learn from failure, and experiment again.

> THE GRATEFUL DEAD TEACHES US TO TAKE RISKS AND TO EXPERIMENT, TO LEARN FROM OUR FAILURES AND SUCCESSES, AND TO CONTINUALLY MOVE FORWARD.

Marketers should shorten up their planning cycles to monthly—versus six to twelve months out—in order to become more agile in response to changing marketplace dynamics, new product developments, changing competitive landscapes, and new marketing technologies. It may feel natural to be in a yearly planning cycle since it makes people feel more organized, but, for marketers, the cycles should be short and agile to make room for experiments, fast failures, and nimble reactions.

DROPBOX "LEARNS EARLY, LEARNS OFTEN"

Launched in 2008, Dropbox is a service that lets people easily share files across their own computers, eliminating the need to lug your machine from home to the office or to have to move files on USB sticks.

To promote their product, Dropbox used traditional "best practice" tactics for their industry, including a launch at the TechCrunch 50, running lots of pay-per-click campaigns, and hiring a traditional PR firm to "get the word out."

The result? Expensive failure—to the tune of $233 to $388 spent per each new customer who bought a $99 product. Ouch! Instead of giving up or throwing more money at the problem, the Dropbox team went back to the drawing board.

The team realized that despite losing money on acquiring new customers, existing customers were referring new customers at interesting rates. Because the product was so easy to use and solved a problem, people were talking about it and sharing it with others. Dropbox also learned that while pay per click search is a great way to harvest demand, it's not the way to create it. In other words, marketing tactics that work for an existing market can utterly fail for a new market.

Using this information, Dropbox experimented with new tools for increasing online referrals. One thing that worked was allowing people to share folders within their product, which further increased product exposure within user networks. In addition they made it very easy for users to refer other people by sending them a link via Facebook/X, by importing contact lists from e-mail systems and sending e-mails, or by individually adding the e-mail addresses of people users wanted to refer. Dropbox also experimented with incentives. Users who refer new users to Dropbox receive free additional storage for each referral.

Dropbox's willingness to be open-minded about how to market their products and to experiment paid off. The company's user base grew from 100,000 users in September 2009 to over 4 million users in January 2010—largely fueled by their clever referral system. Wowsa!

ROCK ON

Run experiments in your marketing department

Like music, marketing is a creative discipline. Instead of worrying about making mistakes, you should be doing at least five times more experiments than you are likely doing today. In terms of marketing, this could mean experimenting with AI, freeing your employees to start a TikTok channel or write for your blog (or comment on others' blogs). You could start your own weekly podcast or video channel or create a new tool that gives people information they can use in their day-to-day jobs. The key to all of this is that you learn from your mistakes!

ACTION: Reframe your planning cycle in your company. It is okay to have an annual marketing budget, but plan your activities in monthly "sprints" in which you execute your projects for 19 days a month, spend one day a month learning from the previous months' projects, and then selecting the next month's projects. When you pick your projects for the next month, make sure that at least 20 percent of them are purely experimental.

CHAPTER 6
Embrace Technology

You may not expect it from a bunch of carefree guys who just want to play music, but the Grateful Dead has been pushing the technological boundaries of music for decades. The legendary concert experience—which inspired people to drop out of conventional society and follow the band from city to city—included customized setups so elaborate that the band had to invent the systems, because there was nowhere to buy the technology infrastructure.

Rolled out for the first time in 1974, the Wall of Sound took eight years of experimentation, $350,000 to create, and used 26,400 watts of power from fifty-five McIntosh 2300 amplifiers. It was so far ahead of any other rock band's concert sound system, it catapulted the Grateful Dead into a different music-technology solar system. "The Wall" was also a visual work of art, including over 600 speakers (88 JBL fifteen-inch, 174 JBL twelve-inch, 288 JBL five-inch, and fifty-four ElectroVoice tweeters) in a huge geometric pattern that caused concertgoers to literally gasp when they first saw the setup.

Throughout the decades, technology has continued to be an essential element of live shows. For example, in the 1980s a $30,000 harmonic analyzer originally designed by NASA to evaluate the aerodynamic strength of metals was added to the live show equipment.

> THE TECHNOLOGY DEPLOYED BY THE GRATEFUL DEAD AT LIVE SHOWS ENHANCED THE BAND'S MUSICAL CREATIVITY, MAKING THEM THE MOST SUCCESSFUL TOURING BAND IN HISTORY.

The band continues to innovate, using technology to facilitate the culture of openness and availability they have carefully cultivated over decades. In 2015, Grateful Dead members Bob Weir, Bill Kreutzmann, and Mickey Hart teamed up with John Mayer, Oteil Burbridge, and Jeff Chimenti as Dead & Company, continuing the tradition of innovation. Dead & Company, with Jay Lane replacing Bill Kreutzmann, were among the first bands to play at Sphere Las Vegas in 2024, the most technically advanced music venue in the world, which features 580,000 sq feet of LEDs and 1,586 permanently installed speakers plus 300 mobile modules.

At each stage of the band's development, the Grateful Dead challenged and pushed to the limit what was possible based on the technology of the day. In the 1970s it was live concert technology in 2009 it was a real-time iPhone application, and in 2025 an immersive sound and light experience.

Marketing Lesson from the Grateful Dead
Embrace Technology

Of course, it's not just music and not just the Dead. We're living in a Communications Revolution driven by advancements in marketing technology. With the explosion of new ways for people to communicate using real-time networking tools like TikTok, X, and LinkedIn; plus the ability of any organization to become a publisher of podcasts, video channels' and the ability to deploy AI at scale comes pushback within many companies.

Despite the enormous success of the Grateful Dead in pushing the limits of what is possible with available technologies, we see many companies that have yet to catch on with even mainstream technology. At most companies, marketing is a creative discipline, with artistic types dominating soft discussions about branding, image, and slogans. While these elements are important, technology is often pushed aside. Knowledge of technologies like AI, web analytics, marketing optimization, CRM systems, and social media aren't a priority for many of the marketing departments and company executives we encounter.

> THE GRATEFUL DEAD TEACHES US THAT EMBRACING TECHNOLOGY ENHANCES THE CREATIVE PROCESS AND DRIVES SUCCESS TO THE HIGHEST LEVELS.

Rather than embracing technology, many organizations actively discourage communications that use new technologies. Executives, Human Resources professionals, lawyers, and marketing executives insist that new forms of communications are a time-waster, not "real marketing," and even dangerous (because people might, *gasp*, say "bad things").

We've asked hundreds of companies about their use of social technologies and have observed that roughly 25 percent of companies we've encountered actually block employee access to YouTube, Facebook, and other social networking sites. That is a huge number of companies that are putting their organizations at a disadvantage.

Companies tell us that they block access to these sites for two main reasons: It is a drain to productivity and it may harm the company brand should employees reveal too much information.

EMBRACE TECHNOLOGY AT THE
U.S. DEPARTMENT OF DEFENSE

Even the U.S. Department of Defense embraces communications technologies, much like The Dead. In early 2010, the DoD released its official policy covering new media technologies. With some three million employees, the DoD is one of the largest organizations in the world, so this was big news.

The policy, Directive-Type Memorandum 09-026, which was effective immediately, states that DoD employees (including the U.S. Army, Air Force, Navy, and Marines) can use and participate in new media and social networking sites such as X, Facebook, YouTube, blogs, and forums. Prior to the directive, there were restrictions placed on certain technologies within some service branches.

The DoD understands that it's not about controlling the technology anymore. It's about giving people who work in the armed services access to technology so they can communicate in the ways that their peers, friends, family members, and general public demand.

Now, service members within the U.S. Army, Air Force, Navy, and Marines may make most of their information freely available, serving to market those organizations to people both abroad and at home. What's fascinating about the DoD Social Media Policy is how far out in front the military is, compared to many corporations. The U.S. military is using marketing lessons from the Grateful Dead! (What would Jerry Garcia think?)

Instead of blocking access to social media sites, company executives need to understand that this is the way people communicate in 2010. People are able to better maintain relationships on Facebook and LinkedIn. They share what they are up to on X and TikTok, and publish valuable information on YouTube and blogs.

ROCK ON

Develop your company's Artificial Intelligence guidelines

It's not only huge organizations like the DoD that need technology policies and guidelines. All organizations (even those with a handful of people) should have a set so that the people within those organizations understand how to best use technology including AI.

ACTION: Develop guidelines for your organization.

Assemble a team composed of appropriate stakeholders (executives, human resources department, legal staff, PR people, and others) and study available guidelines from other organizations. Often you can find these documents online. From there you can craft your own set of AI and technology guidelines, appropriate for your company. Publish the guidelines for all employees to see and talk up the use of technology to develop a culture around its use.

Chapter 7
Establish a New Category

Go to Spotify and you'll find 6,291 genres of music: Some have remained constant for years like pop, rap, and rock. Many are newer like modern Bollywood or alternative metal. Most bands and their music fit into one or several of these categories: Led Zeppelin is "Rock" while Bob Marley is "Reggae." The Grateful Dead, on the other hand, defied existing category boundaries by combining various genres of music and melding it all with extreme improvisation to create their own unique sound—and in the process, their own musical category.

Early in the band's history, the Grateful Dead teamed up with Ken Kesey and provided music for his Acid Tests, elaborate parties where the participants dropped acid. The Acid Tests weren't concerts where people came and watched the band perform; rather, the audience members were expected to be part of the performance and provide entertainment to the other attendees. This tradition of the crowd being part of the performance continued long after the Grateful Dead grew beyond being Kesey's house band. A big part of the Grateful Dead's value proposition was not just what was happening on stage, but the collective experience you had being entertained by the audience, with whom you were having a unique, collective experience.

From those early days, the Grateful Dead became known for their extended riffs and improvisational jams, which often melded jazz, country, bluegrass, psychedelic, and rock. Because the resulting fusion of genres defied set categories, the band's followers came up with a new category, "Jam Band," a term now used to classify bands, such as Phish and Goose, that followed in the Grateful Dead's footsteps.

> THE GRATEFUL DEAD CROSSED MUSICAL BOUNDARIES AND CREATED THEIR OWN SOUND—SETTING THEMSELVES APART FROM OTHER BANDS.

By innovating across musical boundaries, the Grateful Dead stood out from other bands of their time—the Rolling Stones, the Beatles, and so on—a uniqueness they carried with them throughout their career.

The Grateful Dead attracted fans who took to the road, following the band across the United States and creating an entire subculture that included its own language (i.e., "space," "drums," "tapers"), traditions, fashions, and "alternative" lifestyle. Beyond the music, this subculture and the fans themselves became part of the product that attracted new fans.

Marketing Lesson from the Grateful Dead
Establish a New Category

In every industry, there is a barely distinguishable herd of competitors that move in unison. Don't fall into the trap of moving in lockstep with that herd. Rather than try to outperform your competition in your existing industry, follow the Grateful Dead's recipe and create a new industry by reconstructing your market's boundaries.

The problem with innovating within industry boundaries is that you end up spending huge sums of money trying to move the needle a few percentage points in terms of market share. When a boundary-changing newcomer comes along, companies and their mildly differentiated products lose tremendous market share and sometimes die—as seen when Blockbuster reacted too late to competition from the Web, broadband, and the "content-on-demand" services provided by cable companies and Netflix.

> The Grateful Dead teaches us that ignoring conventional wisdom is the key to creating uncontested market spaces.

Y COMBINATOR CREATES A NEW INVESTOR CATEGORY

The most anxiety-inducing part of any start-up is raising money from angel investors and venture capitalists (VCs). This process creates problems for founders, for four reasons. One, founders spend a great deal of time wooing angel investors and VCs—time that could be spent building a product or selling to customers. Two, investors and VCs often give founders more money than is needed in the early stages of the business, which means more dilution for the founders. Three, investors insist on getting "preferred" stock, which has stronger rights than the founders' stock. And four, in order to "watch" their investment, outside investors want seats on the board and will make business decisions for the founders. Often these problems are so great that the start-up ends up not getting funding or falling apart after it gets funding.

Serial entrepreneur Paul Graham saw these problems and decided to change the experience by providing seed funding for start-ups by using a novel approach through his new company Y Combinator. First, instead of going through the dog-and-pony show that's typical of the investor wooing process, start-ups looking for seed money simply click a link to a short online application from Y Combinator and fill it out. Y Combinator then invites the most promising founders in for a meeting and makes its funding decisions immediately after, dramatically reducing the time a founder needs to spend on raising money and dramatically increasing the time the founder can spend on building a great product or signing up early customers.

Instead of investing in companies one at a time, Y Combinator invests in two "batches" per year with many companies per batch. Because this batch size is large, Y Combinator invests a smaller amount of money than a typical angel or VC. In many industries, the costs associated with starting a business have dropped, so the smaller amount of money is just enough to "prove the concept" and, after that, the company will either keep going or shut down. The typical Y Combinator investment dilutes the founder 2 percent to 10 percent—as opposed to the typical 20 percent to 50 percent associated with angels or VCs. Y Combinator also buys the same type of stock as the entrepreneurs (common as opposed to preferred) with far fewer strings attached.

And finally, rather than take a board seat from which to "watch" the investment, Y Combinator requires all of the recipients to come to San Francisco where the founders are groomed through a series of one-to-many seminars and bootcamps over two months, a process likened to a start-up business degree. This bootcamp format is great for the young entrepreneurs they fund and is just the right level of involvement.

Like the Grateful Dead and its music, slapping the "VC" or "angel investor" label on Y Combinator is difficult because what it offers is so different from what the typical VC or angel investor offers entrepreneurs wanting to start a company. Y Combinator has ignored traditional market boundaries and has created its own category!

ROCK ON

Redefine your industry boundaries

Every industry has opportunities for creating new ways of doing business that can separate your company from your competition and place you in your own unique category. Just as Y Combinator put some real thought into how VC and angel funding wasn't helping start-ups, and thus created a completely new category that is being followed by new groups like Techstars, you, too, must develop a similar approach to your industry.

ACTION: Redefining your industry boundaries is not an easy task. Rather than try to tell you how to do it, we will pose some questions for you to ask yourself to get your ideas flowing.

In addition to thinking about your industry competitors, what are the "alternatives" to your product? Can you find ways to erase the traditional "boundaries" of your industry by incorporating or subsuming or competing with some of the alternatives?

PART TWO
THE FANS

Chapter 8
Encourage Eccentricity

If you'd been to a Grateful Dead concert before, you would understand the unusual experience. The casual approach, beginning the show without fanfare. The lack of a Billboard hit song. The warm community vibe. The thick smoke from a thousand joints. A live Grateful Dead show was unlike anything else in the music world. The eccentricity of the whole thing seemed oddly comfortable and satisfying.

But to a newbie, the scene, and the concert itself, prompted many questions and comments: "Why don't they tune up before they come onto the stage?" "The guitarist is wearing shorts." "Two drummers?" "Really? They take a half-hour break in the middle of the show?" "That song lasted 17 minutes!" And then, of course, there was the sheer wonder at what went down at the park across from the arena all afternoon: "Look, tie-dyed socks!" "Why don't the cops arrest all these people smoking dope?" "Everyone is smiling (even the cops); this is such a happy crowd!"

> THROUGH THEIR OWN ECCENTRICITY, THE GRATEFUL DEAD ENCOURAGED ECCENTRICITY IN THEIR FANS, GIVING PEOPLE A CREATIVE OUTLET TO EXPRESS THEMSELVES.

The Grateful Dead tribe was made up of eccentrics who used the live shows as an outlet to express themselves in a supportive atmosphere. To be sure, some diehard fans wore "hippie clothes" year-round, drove a VW bus, and lived on a commune. But the majority of fans would drift into the scene only when the band was in town, leaving the tie-dye clothes hanging in the closet while they went to classes at a prestigious university, worked on a Wall Street bond-trading floor, or wrote stories for a major newspaper. Deadheads are your neighbors, coworkers, and friends. The concerts allowed fans an outlet, a place to relax and rejoice, to dance, mingle, have fun, and, most important, feel comfortable in a supportive atmosphere of like-minded people.

Marketing Lesson from the Grateful Dead
Encourage Eccentricity

As a marketing strategy, the idea of challenging the accepted standards or creating a product that may seem a little weird can make companies highly successful. There will always be various groups who see themselves as different, special even, in their fierce independence. These independent thinkers look for companies and organizations to do business with and search out products to buy that reflect their sense of self. In a world of "me-too" products, the businesses that cultivate a strategy of appealing to the tastes of outliers are generating success.

Your potential customers value uniqueness. And get this—they'll frequently pay more to be different! An Apple computer is much more expensive than its rivals and Apple fans will happily pay the price difference. The Apple marketing team understands deeply the personalities of the people who buy their products. Much like the Grateful Dead, Apple cultivates an enthusiastic fan base. And just as a Grateful Dead concert is different from other rock concerts, an Apple retail store is different too. No cash registers. No clutter. What few shelves exist are tucked away in the back. There's even a "Genius Bar" where helpful employees will guide you in the ways of eccentricity . . . er, Apple.

Still, most companies continue to create products as direct competitors to established players in the market. Instead of catering to those who wish to be different, they offer products that are exactly the same as the competition. Or they toss out something that's the same but a little cheaper than the other guys.

> THE GRATEFUL DEAD TEACHES US THAT WE ARE ALL ECCENTRIC IN SOME WAYS. SMART COMPANIES UNDERSTAND ECCENTRICITIES AND CREATE A MARKET FROM THEM.

Eccentrics take on many forms. When everyone else is carrying nylon computer bags and sporty backpacks to the office, the eccentric insists on an "old-fashioned" leather briefcase. The eccentric spends six hours on a beautiful Saturday afternoon in a dingy rec room playing Dungeons and Dragons. The eccentric collects chewing gum wrappers and has over 2,000, with examples from over 50 countries. The eccentric reads instead of watching television. The eccentric rides a bike instead of driving. The eccentric is us. And the eccentric is you (after all, you're reading this really weird book on Grateful Dead marketing! What would they think if they knew?!).

In other words, eccentrics are a huge market.

NEW BELGIUM BREWING COMPANY: FAT AND HAPPY

In the world of beer, the offerings of the huge breweries are fine for the masses. Most people are perfectly happy sipping a cold one from the likes of Anheuser–Busch InBev or Miller-Coors. But the eccentric is looking for something different. Much different. Something like Fat Tire Amber Ale from New Belgium Brewing Company in Fort Collins, Colorado. Fat Tire was named in honor of New Belgium founder Jeff Lebesch's bike trip through Belgium, visiting breweries. He learned about the way Belgian beers use a broader palette of ingredients (fruits, spices, esoteric yeast strains) than German or English styles. Fat Tire won fans who appreciate the interesting taste (as well as those who are drawn to the quirky name).

To encourage the eccentric fans who enjoy Fat Tire Amber Ale, New Belgium sponsors an annual "Tour de Fat" bicycle parade and festival. Here is the information about the 2010 Tour de Fat:

> Yes folks, the Tour de Fat will once again be meandering and pandering through 13 western cities spreading the good word about the positive societal offerings of the bicycle. Along with our exceptional ability to roust a city's inner-cyclist, in 2010 we hope

to drive our message even deeper by bringing you the biggest, most enjoyable traveling bike festival that we know of. May the revival roll forth in the name of the bicycle, and may you ride true to The Ten Commandments of the Tour de Fat:

1. Put no means of transport before thy bike
2. Honor all other bikes
3. May every generation come forth
4. Thou shall come as a participant, not a spectator
5. Thou shalt not bring booze
6. New Belgium shalt not profit
7. Remember the purpose, and bring not your pooches
8. Keep the day true with thy good juju
9. Thou shall rise early
10. Thou shalt not steal thy neighbors' bike

Like the Grateful Dead, New Belgium Brewing Company has built a vibrant community for lovers of Fat Tire Amber Ale and the brewery's other brands. The community of eccentrics comes together for physical events (like the Tour de Fat) and tours of the "Liquid Center" (the brewery). And the company also encourages its eccentrics to "Follow our folly" on social networking sites. By creating products (and a community) for eccentrics, New Belgium Brewing Company has grown quickly from its beginnings in 1991.

ROCK ON

Cultivate eccentrics

Have you noticed that people who are passionate about something are eager to talk it up, just like fans of the Grateful Dead want to talk up their favorite band? Your job is to create an experience that's unique, one that eccentrics will gravitate to, and one that they want to talk up.

ACTION: Build personality into your web site. Remove any content that looks similar to your competitors'. Delete what's boring. Make sure your web site, blog posts, newsletters, and e-mails are unlike all others in the marketplace. Being unique will make you stand out. Build up the information (videos, blog posts, e-books, and photos) that appeals to eccentrics in your marketplace.

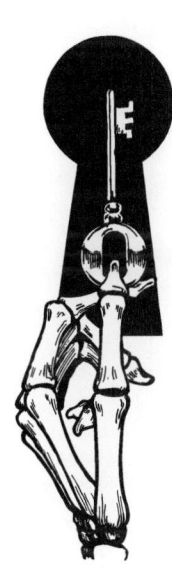

Chapter 9
Bring People on an Odyssey

From their earliest beginnings in the mid-1960s, the Grateful Dead was creating a community of music fans that came to be known as Deadheads. Band members Jerry Garcia, Phil Lesh, Bob Weir, Bill Kreutzmann, and Ron "Pigpen" McKernan lived together at 710 Ashbury Street in San Francisco in the early years, and there were always people from the Haight-Ashbury neighborhood stopping by, hanging out, partying. During these formative years the band would perform many free gigs in the San Francisco area, making music they enjoyed and were thrilled to share with their friends. The fledgling community started coming together.

After their first album, *The Grateful Dead,* released by Warner Bros. in March 1967, the band embarked on a national tour (including their first gigs in New York City) to promote the album. With each new audience came new fans from across the country. With this rise in popularity, the band began wondering how they would bring the new fans into the spiritual community they had created back home. A notice placed inside the October 1971 live *Skull and Roses* album solved the problem:

DEAD FREAKS UNITE:
Who are you? Where are you? How are you?
Send us your name and address and we'll keep you informed.
Deadheads, P.O. Box 1065, San Rafael, California 94901.

A few times a year newsletters were sent out to the list of addresses they collected announcing tour dates and providing news about the extended family that was the Grateful Dead (including such things as individual band members solo projects, wedding and birth announcements from the road and office crew, and the like). But what the mailing list really did was to bring thousands of people together into a pre-Web social network. The fans could opt in, connect with each other at shows, share common interests, be informed of upcoming events, feel like they were part of a community. It was like Facebook before Mark Zuckerberg was even born. Later, the mailing list was converted to e-mail and reached a half million subscribers by the mid-1990s.

Deadheads love the music, of course. But the Grateful Dead community is also about much more: friendship; growing up together; sharing a strong musical and spiritual bond. Hundreds of people even followed the band from city to city over the several months of a tour. This core group would travel in a wide assortment of vehicles (including the now famous VW microbus), hang out in the parking lot of each venue, and find somewhere to camp at night. Fans have been attending shows with some of the same people for more than 20 years—catching up over beers before the concert or during set breaks—following the sagas of each others' careers, kids, and marriages (and a few divorces). While the Grateful Dead delivered good musical vibes, the traveling caravan was a trek, an adventure to be shared with friends. And while we maintained old friendships at shows, new ones were quickly developed, as strangers became friends in the supportive Deadhead environment.

> THE GRATEFUL DEAD LET THEIR AUDIENCE DEFINE THE GRATEFUL DEAD EXPERIENCE. THEY MADE FANS AN EQUAL PARTNER IN A MUTUAL JOURNEY.

Fans of the Grateful Dead know what we're talking about as we describe the mutual journey and close bond that a shared Grateful Dead experience brings. Here are a few examples of some of our memorable encounters. If you are a Deadhead, you've got your own experiences. If you are new to the band, we hope these help to give a taste of what memories people have.

March 2, 1981, Ohio: David is driving with friends from Kenyon College up Interstate 71 on the way to a Grateful Dead gig at Cleveland Music Hall. They stop at a remote rest area. There David runs into his friend Jim from Connecticut, whom he hasn't seen for a year. Jim is also trekking up to the show with *his* college friends (from Ohio Wesleyan). The Grateful Dead brought us together unexpectedly, making our mutual ties to the band even stronger. The random encounter is perfect, cosmic, generating smiles and hugs, and a warm glow inside. The band renews ties to people who would not see one another under normal circumstances.

October 11, 1983, New York City: David's first job after graduating from college is on a Wall Street bond-trading desk.

He's excited because he's meeting his friend Mason at Madison Square Garden to see the Grateful Dead. But David is a very junior employee and doesn't want to attract attention, so he doesn't tell anyone where he's going after work. David and Mason are both in suits at the show (fairly common at a city show on a weeknight in the 1980s and 1990s). But then David sees a colleague, a well-respected trader who is so senior that David has never spoken directly to him. He's in jeans and tie-dye. *"You're a Deadhead?"* They both laugh, high five one another, and from then on they become friends over the shared interest. It's sort of like a secret society, a shared interest in something that others in the office don't know about. The band creates and then cements ties between people that wouldn't normally exist.

April 18, 2009, Worcester, MA: After years of hearing the music on long car rides, David brings his wife and teenage daughter to their very first Dead show. He scored seventh-row tickets through the Grateful Dead ticketing office. At the intermission, both wife and daughter are having a great time and both want T-shirts. But then, hey, there's Brian! He's in the third row with his friends. They meet and share the bond of Deadheads everywhere.

Marketing Lesson from the Grateful Dead
Bring People on an Odyssey

A Grateful Dead concert was about having fun, meeting friends, checking out great music, escaping the everyday, belonging. Each person defined the experience a little differently, and the group defined the whole. At concerts of many other bands (the Rolling Stones come to mind), the rock gods are on stage in flashy costumes, delivering identically flawless shows each night. Sure, shows from other bands are also fun, but the musicians are stars. The Grateful Dead looked like us. They acted like us. They made mistakes. Sometimes they had bad nights. The audience loved it when the Grateful Dead made an obvious error on stage. When there was a missed lyric, the audience and musicians shared a chuckle. Just like each of us, the band was imperfect, so we felt a special brotherhood you just can't replicate when you see Mick Jagger strutting on stage.

There were interesting subgroups wandering along as part of the larger odyssey that was the Grateful Dead experience. At many shows you saw Deaf Heads, people who could not hear the music but felt it through balloons that they held in front of them. As one would expect from a community as inclusive as Deadheads, many people who were not hearing-impaired learned how to sign "hello" to their fellow travelers. Spinners, another subgroup, enjoyed finding a bit of open space in the venue to spin, and spin . . . and spin . . . in ecstasy to the music. It was a common sight that brought smiles to everyone's faces. The band noticed the Spinners and began installing speakers in the concourse area of the concert arenas so the spinners could enjoy quality sound, too, making Spinners true traveling companions on the odyssey instead of outliers.

Marketing Lessons from the Grateful Dead

> THE GRATEFUL DEAD TEACHES US THAT OUR COMMUNITY DEFINES WHO WE ARE. COMPANIES CANNOT FORCE A MINDSET ON THEIR CUSTOMERS.

In building a community, the Grateful Dead were willing to give up a large degree of control over how they were defined and instead handed it to their fans. While this approach is highly unusual, it is also often very successful. When organizations insist on operating in a command-and-control environment with mission statements, boilerplate descriptions, messaging processes, and PR campaigns, their strategies can both hamper growth and backfire in execution.

THE ODYSSEY OF ... SNOWBOARDS

After fooling around with a "Snurfer," a smallish surfboard for the snow with a rope handle, Jake Burton had an idea. He adapted the Snurfer concept, installed bindings for ski boots, and created the first-ever snowboard. In 1977, as interest in snowboarding exploded, Burton built the world's first snowboard factory in Vermont. But rather than just building a company, Burton took a lesson from the Grateful Dead and created a community, taking customers on what's been an over-30-year odyssey. In the early days of snowboarding, riders were barred from using the chairlifts at "skiers only" resorts. Burton and his fledgling community of snowboard enthusiasts pressed on and soon mountains like Suicide Six,

Stratton, and Stowe began granting the new sport's enthusiasts equal access to the slopes in the early 1980s.

What started as an underground, grassroots business was spread around the world by a passionate group of riders who created a community. The early success of the U.S. Open Snowboarding Championships, started in 1982 for snowboarders, by snowboarders, further helped legitimize the sport and increase acceptance among mountain resorts.

Thirty-three years later, Burton not only owns the world's leading snowboard company, he also still rides as much as possible. He's on the snow at least 100 days a year (about the same number of days per year that the Grateful Dead was on tour for several decades). He tests new Burton products, takes runs with fellow riders, and, most important, has fun. Like the Deadheads, the snowboarding community grew quickly as enthusiasts spread the word far and wide. The sport gained true acceptance when snowboarding premiered at the 1998 Nagano Olympics, with several riders winning medals on Burton boards.

While Burton has dedicated his life to snowboarding and played a vital role in transitioning snowboarding from a backyard hobby to a household name, it was the community that turned it into a mainstream sport. At first it was just a few thousand enthusiasts talking up the new sport. Soon millions of people around the world eagerly shared their excitement with friends, colleagues, and family members. Snowboarder Shaun White, who rides Burton Snowboards, is one of the most recognized athletes in the world.

ROCK ON

Lose control of your marketing messages

If you're to build a base of dedicated fans who will join you on an odyssey of success, you will need to lose control. Let your community define you, rather than trying to dictate what's said and how about your company. For example, you could work with bloggers, people who create and post videos onto YouTube, and other people active in social media. If you have a product or service that lends itself to providing free samples, find people to share it with and let them write about you. Or invite podcasters to your company to meet with staff or have an interview with your CEO or product designer. When you let others define and talk about you, it is more likely that a community will develop. And by all means when a community does develop (like the "spinners" at a Dead show), embrace what they have created and help it along (like the band did when they installed speakers for the spinners).

You can also get out into the marketplace and interact with the community as equals. Like Jake Burton and the Grateful Dead, both David and

Brian also spend around 100 days each year with our community—we speak at events, participate in discussions, and appear on podcasts.

ACTION: Remove made-up, gobbledygook-laden mission statements, boilerplate press releases, and other top-down messaging from your materials and web sites. Instead, point people to your community: the conferences, forums, chat rooms, and blogs of the people who talk you up. Then get out into your community and interact regularly.

Chapter 10
Put Fans in the Front Row

If you're like us, you've been to concerts by many rock bands besides the Grateful Dead. Back in the day (prior to the Web), getting tickets for popular shows meant standing in line hours before the 10:00 A.M. on-sale time at the Ticketron outlet in your hometown. Or you could try your luck by calling the telephone number at 10:00, hoping you could get through and that tickets were available by the time you got off hold to speak to a representative. For popular bands, electronic ticketing meant that ticket scalpers would end up with the best seats, while fans often couldn't get tickets at all. This made it nearly impossible for the true fans to get up front at shows.

Unlike nearly every other band, the Grateful Dead controlled the ticket sales for their concerts. While other bands moved toward selling tickets through electronic systems of the day, like Ticketron and, later, Ticketmaster, the Grateful Dead established their own in-house ticketing agency in the early 1980s.

The unique ticketing system of the Grateful Dead led to word-of-mouth marketing like this: "Want some great seats to the Grateful Dead concert? You can buy tickets directly from the band. I know their phone number!"

Fans would call a special telephone number to hear a recording about the upcoming tour and then mail in ticket requests, along with money orders, directly to the Grateful Dead ticketing office in San Rafael, California. The best seats were then mailed to those in the know, the fans who knew the drill and were motivated to go to the post office, get a money order, and follow the ticket request procedures. For most gigs, blocks of tickets were also sold at the venue box office and through the electronic ticketing systems. But the best seats always went to the band's biggest fans.

> THE GRATEFUL DEAD ANNOUNCED TOURS TO FANS FIRST AND TREATED SUPPORTERS TO THE BEST SEATS, DRIVING PASSIONATE LOYALTY.

We've used this ticket system many times, both in the Grateful Dead days as well as for tickets to recent shows by The Dead, Furthur, Ratdog, and Phil Lesh & Friends. There's something special about feeling like you are in the know. These days, in our plugged-in world, tour announcements are made on a web site (www.gdtstoo.com) and via broadcast e-mail, but the ticketing procedures are the same.

When your self-addressed envelope from the ticket office arrives, there was an excitement and feeling of being part of an elite group. The much-anticipated package holds a mystery. Where will I be sitting? Did I score this time?

Grateful Dead tickets were allotted based on postmark plus other mysterious factors that nobody could quite figure out. We've been buying since the beginning and aren't really sure how they allocate seats. Is it random? Do they know how many tickets we've bought over the years? How much does a clever drawing on the envelope help get us up front? Most of the time, it seems like the luck of the draw.

Sometimes you get great seats. Sometimes they are a bit further back, but you are always in better seats than the second-class citizens who purchased through Ticketmaster. A few times we've gotten front row center seats! Imagine the feeling a fan gets when she opens an envelope to find those choice seats. It is that commitment to the fans that helped drive a passionate community, loyal to the band, for decades.

Marketing Lesson from the Grateful Dead
Put Fans in the Front Row

The Grateful Dead teaches us to treat customers with care and respect. Yet we see so many organizations that do precisely the opposite. Instead of putting loyal customers first, they ignore them while they try to get new ones. While we're all for growing a business, we don't think it should come at the expense of annoying existing customers.

Always remember, your most passionate fans are also the people who tell your stories and spread your ideas. Your most passionate fans are those who will continue to come back to your company year after year.

> **THE GRATEFUL DEAD TEACHES US TO TREAT CUSTOMERS WITH CARE AND RESPECT.**

Think about the many companies you do business with that flaunt their new customer offers. How much sense does it make to offer a new subscriber to a magazine a rate of $39.99 a year when a loyal existing subscriber must pay $99.95 for the same product? How about the cable television company offering the first three months of service free? Or they offer the first year at a discount, but if you decide to be loyal to the company and renew, your rates actually increase. With offers like these, companies routinely alienate their most loyal supporters.

But it's not only the pricing model that's crucial. The Grateful Dead always announced ticket availability to their fans first. They built loyalty because people knew that the way to get the inside track on the upcoming show schedule was to stay in tune with the band.

How many companies do you know that tell the media about their newest offering first? How often do you learn about the newest model of the car you loyally drive from a newspaper or magazine instead of the automaker or dealer? We wonder why automakers don't contact their existing customers with an offer of an exclusive test drive of the hot new model.

And it's not only automakers who ignore loyal customers, we see this behavior in many different industries.

Companies need to flip-flop the way they do business. Give your best deals to existing customers. Tell your fans first. Show the people who invest their time and money in your company that you care.

OBAMA FOR AMERICA AND PUTTING FANS FIRST

It was Saturday, August 23, 2008, and U.S. presidential candidate Barack Obama was set to announce his choice of running mate. Conventional PR rules would suggest that the Obama for America campaign issue a press release and let the television channels, newspapers, news web sites, and other outlets of mainstream media break the news in real time.

But that's not what the Obama campaign did.

Instead, the candidate announced the news to fans first, via IM, e-mail, and this tweet from the candidate's X feed at @BarackObama: "Announcing Senator Joe Biden as our VP nominee. Watch the first Obama-Biden rally live at 3 P.M. ET on http://BarackObama.com." Supporters learned of the Biden nod ten minutes before mainstream media. The Obama campaign alerted their most important supporters first! (Of course, smart journalists could have subscribed to the @BarackObama X feed or e-mail list to get the news, too.)

It was this kind of attention to the most ardent supporters that helped get Obama elected. This idea of connecting with your most important constituents first (and offering them the best deal) is an important lesson straight from the Grateful Dead's playbook.

An interesting aside to bring this story full circle: The Dead played at one of newly elected President Obama's inauguration galas in Washington, D.C.

ROCK ON

Create exclusive programs for your most loyal supporters

Every organization should be thinking about how to cultivate its most loyal supporters and treat them as special. This approach need not be as formalized as the airline frequent flyer programs. Many times, simply alerting existing customers first with news and announcements is enough. Certainly, all companies should rethink the common practice used with telecommunications companies, newspapers, and magazines of offering cheaper rates new subscribers than to current ones.

ACTION: Identify your most loyal customers and add them to a database so that you can reach them. What can you offer them that would be valuable and not available to the general public?

Communicate to this loyal group first. Before your next product release, do a special event, teleconference, or webinar for your existing customers. Let them know first, before you alert the media and other constituents.

CHAPTER 11
Build a Following

Word-of-mouth was a very important factor in increasing the Grateful Dead fan base. Friends told friends who told friends, which spread the word and swelled the fan base, but in those pre-Web days, how did the band keep fans apprised of concert dates, news, and other Grateful Dead happenings? It's a great question, given that fans today can easily learn the latest Dead news with just a few clicks to the band's official web site and chat forums, Facebook fan page, and X feed.

From the outside, the Grateful Dead looked like they didn't have a clue about business, but in reality, they were forward-looking, especially when it came to building their database and connecting with their fans—a lesson companies today can readily apply.

In 1968 the band hired the Grateful Dead fan Scott Brown as an album production coordinator. In addition to his day job, Brown also manned a booth at all the Grateful Dead shows where he signed up thousands of fans who wanted to receive updates about the band and their tours. As we mention earlier in the book, the Grateful Dead also placed its "Dead Freaks Unite!" notice on the inside sleeve of the "Skull and Roses" album in 1971, marking the beginning of the Grateful Dead Fan Club and growing the mailing list.

At the time, it was a radical idea for a band to add a "call to action" to an album as an overt way to build their mailing list—and by extension, their following. Six months after running the notice, the band had 10,257 names on their list, including 885 from Europe. The Grateful Dead soon hired Eileen Law to manage the band's burgeoning mailing list. Five years later, the list had grown to 63,147 names in the United States alone—sorted by name and zip code. (And this was before personal computers!)

The band not only reached out to fans, but fans reached out to the band by sending in letters, postcards, and artwork. Law, the "keeper of stuff," saved almost all of this correspondence, much of which is now at the Grateful Dead Archive at U.C. Santa Cruz.

> THE GRATEFUL DEAD WERE EARLY ADOPTERS, FOR THEIR INDUSTRY, OF DATABASE MARKETING TECHNIQUES.

Starting in the 1970s, the band sent out newsletters and other mailings two to three times a year. Early newsletters were typed by hand on an IBM Selectric typewriter and included personal letters to fans.

In May 1974, the band sent fans a one-page letter alerting them to the *From the Mars Hotel* album release and exhorting them to call radio stations: "We know you'll enjoy our album, and if you get real enthused call a radio station or tell a record store. We need all the help we can get."

As the band's fortunes increased, their newsletters became more polished, featuring hand-drawn artwork and articles about the band's doings. The Grateful Dead fed their fans' voracious appetites for any kind of news about the band's members—knowing the smallest details became a point of pride among Deadheads. A February 1980 newsletter gives this insight into the band members and their instruments:

> Jerry and Phil are both playing custom-made guitars by Doug Irwin. Bobby still plays an Ibanez and Billy and Mickey are now playing Sonar rosewood drums and Zildjian cymbals. Brent plays a Hammond B-3 organ and Yamaha electric piano.

And of course, Grateful Dead faithful had the Grateful Dead Hotline. Whenever you called, you heard Law's warm voice giving you updated tour information and concert dates.

Once the Web came into play, the Grateful Dead were once again early adopters, feeding information to Dead-Flames, a Usenet news group, and developing the official Grateful Dead web site and an e-mail newsletter.

Marketing Lesson from the Grateful Dead
Build a Following

If you're a marketer or business owner, you've heard the adage that your in-house database is a goldmine. Yet we've both seen how companies mishandle this asset: names of people interested in the company's products or service are collected at a trade show, put in a file folder and filed away in a drawer somewhere . . . to be forgotten. Or, a company adds a subscription form to its web site, but never sends the people who enter their name and e-mail address any type of information—ever. Even worse, a company dumps names and e-mail addresses into their database and begins sending impersonal and unsolicited e-mails—and making recipients angry in the process.

> THE GRATEFUL DEAD TEACHES US TO KEEP IN TOUCH WITH OUR CUSTOMERS ON A PERSONAL LEVEL AND TO USE THE NEWEST TECHNOLOGIES AVAILABLE TO REACH OUT TO THEM.

The Grateful Dead understood that their mailing list was a valuable asset, and they used it to keep their fans informed, to build community, and to let fans know their concert schedule. Just as the Grateful Dead were innovative in the way they built their following by directly communicating with fans via their mail list, you, too, should be similarly innovative in how you build your company's following.

Building a following today requires much more than simply collecting names and e-mail addresses. You need to collect telephone numbers SMS, X followers, Facebook fan page followers, and LinkedIn Group members. You build this following by creating lots of remarkable content that pulls people in—content that's personal, relevant, and interesting to your followers.

In time, your following will dwarf your e-mail list, giving you real leverage. Each time you have a new product or service, you can announce it to larger and larger numbers of people much more efficiently—just as the Grateful Dead did when they grew their fan list by over 500,000 names in five years.

HUBSPOT EXTENDS ITS REACH WITH WEBSITE GRADER

Shortly after its founding, HubSpot, where Brian was CEO, created its Website Grader (www.websitegrader.com), a free tool that analyzes a web site's ability to get found in search engines, blogs, and social media sites and then gives it a grade of 1 to 100 along with some tips on how to improve. A grade of 90 means your site has some mojo while lower scores mean you need some help to increase your ability to get found online. Those who use Website Grader have the option of giving their e-mail address, which HubSpot then adds to its database.

In addition to Website Grader (and similar analysis tools, including XGrader, PressReleaseGrader, and BlogGrader), HubSpot has built its following (or "reach") by offering lots of other free content, including free e-books, white papers, webinars, a blog, a weekly HubSpot TV show, Facebook fan page, and its Inbound Marketing University web site and LinkedIn Group.

HubSpot's efforts have paid off. The company's "reach" in October 2008 was a little over 100,000. By February 2010, that reach had grown to over 500,000, including 33,000-plus followers on X (this does not include individual employees' X followings), 44,000-plus members for the company's Inbound Marketers LinkedIn Group, and 27,000-plus blog subscribers and over 300,000 opt-in e-mail subscribers.

The large reach HubSpot now enjoys brings incredible and ever-growing leverage. When announcing an event such as a webinar for example, they'll send out an e-mail to their list, Tweet about it, announce it on their Facebook fan page and LinkedIn Group—and then watch all of their followers post about the event, too. In October 2008, a promotion reached 100,000 people and by February 2010 it reached 500,000 people. This leverage means that webinar registrations have skyrocketed from about 2,000 to 10,000 people per webinar. As long as its reach continues to grow, HubSpot's leverage in the marketplace grows with it.

ROCK ON

Extend your reach

Like the Grateful Dead, you should be an early adopter in your industry of ways to increase your reach in your marketplace. Since it's not 1990, this means you should stop obsessing over your e-mail database and start enlarging your view of your "reach" by focusing on your blog and podcast subscribers, X followers, Facebook fans, and LinkedIn Group members.

ACTION: Make a chart that shows the total number of names on your e-mail list plus your blog and podcast subscribers, X followers, Facebook fans, and LinkedIn Group members. Update your chart monthly and make it part of your standard reporting and metrics. Create a goal for yourself of growing your overall reach by 5 percent per month.

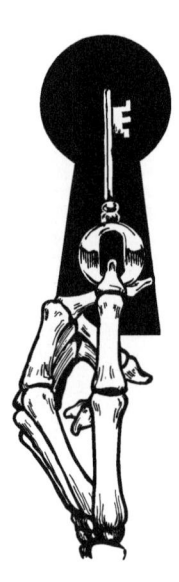

PART THREE
THE BUSINESS

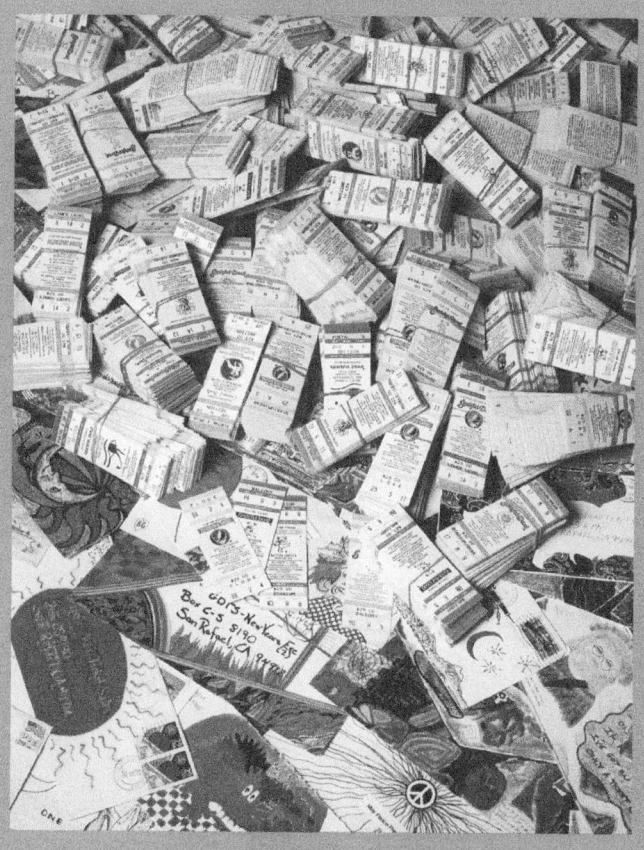

CHAPTER 12
Cut Out the Middleman

Deadheads bought tickets to Grateful Dead shows in a very different way than they did for other concerts. They called into a telephone hotline, which was a voice recording that gave instructions on how to buy tickets directly from the band. The instructions typically involved mailing a self-addressed stamped envelope and a money order for up to four tickets to a Post Office box in San Rafael, California.

So why the heck did the Grateful Dead go through all this trouble rather than just outsourcing this function like every other band? Well, it turns out this process was a brilliant innovation on the Grateful Dead's part from a number of perspectives, including allowing them to control the distribution process start to finish.

By selling tickets directly to fans, the Grateful Dead could keep prices at a level that was affordable to their fans. Rather than let the brokers and scalpers dictate and falsely inflate prices, the band went "direct"—and in doing so ensured that the low-value-add middlemen (brokers and scalpers) couldn't pocket outsized profits from Deadheads off the backs of the Grateful Dead's hard work.

> **THE GRATEFUL DEAD ELIMINATED THE MIDDLEMAN AND SOLD TICKETS DIRECTLY TO FANS.**

Controlling the ticket-ordering process also ensured that the best tickets went to their most loyal fans rather than just to people who had a casual interest. It was a huge pain in the backside to call the hotline repeatedly looking for concert information and then mail a self-addressed envelope with a money order (aaarrrgghh!) than it was to just call Ticketmaster with your credit card. Most businesses optimize for their future potential customers while the Grateful Dead optimized for their current voracious customers.

The ticket distribution process extended the Grateful Dead's authentic brand even further. Rather than deal with a disinterested ticket broker on the phone—the same broker that worked for every other band—you had an authentic, transparent experience when buying tickets directly from the Grateful Dead.

Controlling the ticket-ordering process allowed the Grateful Dead to print their own elaborately decorated tickets—which contrasted sharply from the grey Ticketmaster variety—and cut down on Deadheads getting burned by counterfeiters.

Marketing Lesson from the Grateful Dead
Cut Out the Middleman

Most industries "grew up" with a distribution model that involved a layer or two of middlemen (i.e., brokers) between them and the customer. These layers were necessary because the brokers were "feet on the street" in the local markets and were nearer to the end-customer than the product producer. The Web has flipped this concept on its head. Being located physically near the end-user is much less valuable today than it was traditionally, as you can now reach and service end-customers through the Web much more efficiently. For some industries, having middlemen between the product-maker and the end-user is still important if they are combining your product with other products and services in truly clever ways to add meaningful value. Having said that, in many industries, middlemen are just not adding the same amount of value today that they used to.

> THE GRATEFUL DEAD TEACHES US TO STRIP AWAY THE LAYERS BETWEEN US AND OUR CUSTOMERS AND TO PULL THEM IN DIRECTLY.

If you're starting a new business or you're in a traditional industry with brokers or middlemen, consider these reasons for rethinking your model and going direct, the way the Grateful Dead did.

Going direct allows you to dictate the prices people pay for your products. You really don't want brokers to inflate the prices your customers pay as the demand for almost every product goes down as the price goes up.

The only way to truly determine the demand curve for your product is to try different price points with different customer sets over time to see where the break points are. As a marketer, it's important that you experiment with raising and lowering your prices to figure out the ideal configuration of pricing and packaging in order to maximize profit. When you go through brokers, it limits your ability to experiment with that pricing as it's difficult to get brokers to move their price points around. And, too, they'll often absorb the benefits of any price decrease experiments.

By going direct, you ensure your margins don't get swallowed up by middlemen who insert themselves between you and your customers without adding value that's commensurate with the margin extracted.

GOOGLE ELIMINATES THE NEED FOR MEDIA BROKERS

Before Google Adwords, companies that wanted to purchase TV, radio, newspaper, magazine, and billboard advertising usually went through a media broker. These specialists would put together months-long media buy plans that included dozens of magazines, newspapers, TV, and radio stations.

What made these media brokers necessary to marketers is they knew how to get deep discounts on media buys—discounts a typical marketer couldn't get by simply calling a magazine or newspaper. You then purchased your "buys" three, six, or 12 months in advance and would deliver your ads months or weeks ahead of when the publication printed or the ad spot aired.

The cost of your ad buy was based on the number of readers the publication had or the number of TV show viewers—not whether they actually read or watched your ad and took some sort of action. And, while you had a vague idea who your prospects might be and what they wanted, testing various headlines, copy, calls-to-action, TV spots, and so forth to determine what got their attention could get expensive.

When Google developed its AdWords program, it turned the ad buying process on its ear. Now marketers could purchase advertising directly from the source and pay only if someone took an action—that is, clicking on the ad. Instead of relying on media brokers-as-intermediaries, marketers could create ads in-house, determine the bid rate, and have them online in a matter of minutes.

In addition, Google eliminated the two-tier pricing associated with the media industry (i.e., one price for brokers and another for companies) by offering its transparent bidding platform. Instead of offering multiple tiers, Google takes the same percentage of each "click" whether the company doing the advertising is a big-name brand with a million-dollar budget or a small mom-and-pop spending a few thousand dollars each month.

ROCK ON

Connect directly with your customers

The Web allows you to connect directly with your customers and can help you remove the margin-stripping layers inherent in a distribution channel. As a business owner or marketer, if you can remove these layers, you can increase your margins, increase control of your pricing and demand curve, and increase your authentic transparency with your end-users.

ACTION: If you make a product or service and sell it through brokers or distributors, ask yourself if that construct still makes sense in light of the fact that the Web likely enables you to sell and service your offering much more efficiently (cheaply) than ever before. If you're starting a new business, do not assume that your industry's conventional wisdom about distribution strategy is right, as you might be able to jump over your industry's existing protagonists by skipping the middleman. If you're a broker or middleman yourself, don't wear rose-colored glasses—you had better make sure that you add meaningful, unique value that is well beyond the capabilities of the manufacturer of the product or service that you're distributing.

CHAPTER 13
Free Your Content

Unlike other bands, the Grateful Dead encouraged concert-goers to record their live shows, establishing "taper sections" behind the mixing board where fans' recording gear could be set up for best sound quality. When requesting tickets to a show, a taper would request a seat in the special section reserved just for them.

People attending a Grateful Dead concert for the first time were often surprised to see the forest of professional-grade microphones rising to the sky in the audience. Tapers, as these Deadheads are known, were allowed to freely record Grateful Dead shows using their own equipment. Photography was also encouraged.

Allowing fans to tape concerts was highly unusual as conventional wisdom held that if fans made their own recordings, they wouldn't need to buy records. The Grateful Dead once again rejected conventional wisdom.

The tapers became a subculture within the Grateful Dead community. It was the tapers, more than anything else, who ensured that past performances were captured and shared. Fans poured over these recordings, amassing deep knowledge about performances, including the order of songs played, how each song was played and its length, and the improvisational elements within each one. The tapers became the band's curators and historians.

Rather than prevent their audience from taping their concerts, as every other band did, the Grateful Dead set their music free by allowing and encouraging these tapers. You would have thought that giving their music away would have diminished their success, but setting it free fueled it. Despite the fact that people could get their product for free, the Grateful Dead found themselves playing in larger and larger stadiums as their fan base swelled and, ironically, their generosity fueled album sales, too: 19 gold albums, six platinum, and four multiplatinum.

> THE GRATEFUL DEAD REMOVED BARRIERS TO THEIR MUSIC BY ALLOWING FANS TO TAPE IT, WHICH IN TURN BROUGHT IN NEW FANS AND GREW SALES.

Deadhead fans had been taping shows since the early days—of the over 2,300 shows the Dead played, approximately 2,200 were taped—but as the band's success grew, so did the number of tapers, which caused problems. Concertgoers began complaining of microphones blocking sight lines to the stage.

Rather than ban taping outright or put barriers around it, the Grateful Dead embraced it. In 1984 the band set up its designated taping section behind the mixing board at each concert—to which admission required a special ticket and where fans' recording gear could be set up for the best possible sound quality. In return for sanctioning taping, the band requested that tapers not sell the tapes to others or use them for any commercial purposes.

With the advent of the Web, music fans suddenly had the ability to share music from any band via free download sites such as Napster. The recording industry cracked down, shutting down these sites and making it illegal to download licensed music. The Grateful Dead however, continued its tradition of allowing access to and trading of live recordings. In 1999, the Dead was one of the first bands to allow free downloads (i.e., MP3 files) of their live performances. Since then, Deadheads have grooved to the Grateful Dead on their mobile devices without having to pay for the privilege.

Marketing Lesson from the Grateful Dead
Free Your Content

As we've written before, your marketplace is tired of being marketed to and is getting better and better at blocking interruptions with tools like Caller ID (for phone calls), spam protection (for e-mail blasts), and DVR (for TV ads). So how the heck can you reach your marketplace today if they are blocking your marketing? While your marketplace has stopped listening to your ads, they have fundamentally changed the way they learn about new products. They use AI chatbots, search engines, blogs, and social media sites.

The way to reach your marketplace is to create tons of remarkable, free content like blogs, videos, white papers, and e-books. Giving away free content sounds counter intuitive, but it works. This is because each piece of content you create attracts links in from other web sites. Those links send you traffic and those links inform Google how important you are and move that piece of content up in the rankings.

In other words, each piece of content is like a mini-magnet that attracts potential customers to your business. The really nice thing about these mini-magnets is that they are cumulative. The pieces of content you create never go away as they continue to gain links and rank in the search engines. These mini-magnets behave much like compounding interest in your 401k account.

One comment we frequently hear from smaller companies, especially those that sell a service, is that if you give away your ideas "for free" (i.e., via a blog, white papers, videos, etc.) buyers have no incentive to do business with you. The exact opposite is true: when you give content or small pieces of your product away, it attracts a lot more interest and really opens up the top of your marketing funnel in a dramatic way. The problem you have today is that you don't have enough leads. When you give away some content, you'll have more leads than you know what to do with—along with a much higher "how to qualify" problem!

 THE GRATEFUL DEAD TEACHES US THAT WHEN WE FREE OUR CONTENT, MORE PEOPLE HEAR ABOUT OUR COMPANY AND EVENTUALLY DO BUSINESS WITH US.

Ultimately, the company that regularly produces content and makes it free for the taking sees its revenues grow as "followers" become customers. It worked for the Grateful Dead—and it can work for you, too.

MYSQL OFFERS ITS SOURCE CODE TO DEVELOPERS FOR FREE

MySQL is an open source, database management system used by companies all over the globe, from Sage Accounting and Symantec to Google and the New York Times. Developed by MySQL AB, MySQL was built as an open source software at a time when Microsoft and Oracle dominated the industry with paid, closed-source software. Rather than try and compete with Microsoft and Oracle, MySQL gave away their product and made their money in other ways.

Distributed under the GNU General Public License, anyone could freely use MySQL in their applications with the stipulation that if the company distributed its application, it had to be open source, too. MySQL's freemium business model (where MySQL offered free software but charged for upgraded services) allowed it to grow to more than

10 million downloads a year and about 3,000 to 5,000 leads per day. In addition to the free download, the company also created over 600 pieces of free content, including case studies, a blog, how-to guides, and documentation—all designed to help people use the software as well as pull them in.

So how did the company make money from giving away its product? Companies like Symantec and Sage Accounting were using MySQL in their commercial applications and of course did not want to give away their software, and hence began asking for commercial licenses, which they ended up charging for. Over 80 percent of the company's revenues came from commercial licenses to these OEMs.

In addition, many companies using MySQL needed help with optimizing system uptime and maximizing database performance. Based on this need, MySQL developed a strategy for selling their services and packaging them for enterprises—the resulting software is MySQL Enterprise, which is sold on a subscription basis.

Because they gave the product away for free and upsold the folks who needed extra services, the top of their funnel was gigantic. In turn, their marketing department spent much of their time filtering, scoring, and nurturing leads rather than looking for leads, a good (and rare) problem for a marketing department.

This freemium strategy worked as the company grew from $6 million in revenues in 2003 to $100 million in 2008—when it was sold to Sun Microsystems for $1 billion dollars. Not bad!

ROCK ON

You gotta give to get

Great free stuff acts like a magnet as it both draws people to you and opens up the top of your marketing funnel in a dramatic way. Basically, the freemium model that the Grateful Dead pioneered, and companies like MySQL applied to the software industry, can work in any industry, even yours.

ACTION: Create a great e-book about your industry (not your product) that people will want to share with others. Create a brilliant video about how your industry will evolve over the next 10 years and post it on your blog and on YouTube. Do an industry survey to collect information about some interesting topic and create a remarkable report on it that your industry will love. Build a Web or mobile that will give your market great pleasure (see www.websitegrader.com as an elaborate example). Write a fantastic LinkedIn article once a week about your industry (not your product).

If this content you create is remarkable, it will draw visitors to your business in a far more dramatic way than the product or services page on your web site will ever do.

CHAPTER 14
Be Spreadable

While the tapers who attended and recorded the concerts made up their own mini subculture within the Deadhead community, the fans that collected tapes were a much bigger subculture. Deadheads often had hundreds of tapes in their collections and actively sought recordings of significant shows. Before the Web, people freely passed tapes to friends, who made copies. These friends would share them with their friends, who shared them with their friends, and so on. Deadheads played their tapes in college dorms, at work, and at home—turning on still more fans.

Deadheads also spent hours creating beautifully hand-drawn "covers" for their tapes, especially if a particular show had special meaning (i.e., you met your wife at the concert or your first child was born on that show date). Fans might draw the dancing bears on the tape cover and then give the tape to a friend.

All of this copying and sharing and creating was fully sanctioned by the Grateful Dead, whose only stipulation was that recordings not be sold for commercial purposes.

> **THE GRATEFUL DEAD MADE IT EASY TO SPREAD THEIR MUSIC BECAUSE THEY DIDN'T PLACE BARRIERS AROUND IT.**

The music industry put strict barriers around artists' content, a battle that continues to this day. According to copyright law, a fan could make a copy of an album or a cassette tape but was not supposed to share it with others—the thinking being that sharing would reduce sales. The way you learned about a band's new music was by listening to the radio, talking to friends, or maybe by reading an industry publication such as *Rolling Stone*.

No band freely shared their music with fans the way the Grateful Dead did—and as we've already pointed out, rather than working against them, setting their music free only fueled their success as Deadheads spread their music far and wide. Each tape was like an advertisement that attracted new people to one of their concerts. The more concerts the Grateful Dead performed, the more tapes were in the marketplace. The more copies were made of the tapes, the more advertisements were in the marketplace pulling in new customers.

Marketing Lesson from the Grateful Dead
Be Spreadable

As a marketer, your goal is to spread the word about your product or service in the marketplace. Twenty years ago, the friction in the marketplace was high. To overcome this friction, you spent money on PR firms and on expensive advertising campaigns.

Today, the friction in the marketplace against getting your product known is much, much less. If you have a remarkable idea, you will attract bloggers and social media content creators in your marketplace that will help you propel your idea without spending lots of money on PR and advertising. Like the Grateful Dead, you can set your content free and then watch your fans and followers spread it far and wide.

> THE GRATEFUL DEAD TEACHES US THAT MAKING IT EASY FOR OUR AUDIENCE TO SPREAD OUR CONTENT MAKES OUR PRODUCT "KNOWN" IN THE MARKETPLACE.

Epidemiologists use the term "R-naught" (designated by the symbol R_0) to define the spread of infectious disease outbreaks. Basically, if R_0 is greater than 1, it's an epidemic. If R_0 equals one, it's an epidemic, and if R_0 is less than one, the disease dies out.

You want your content and ideas to have an R_0 as high as possible so that they spread and spread and spread (hence the term "viral" for viral marketing). If 10 people read your content and each person forwards it to at least one person, so that at least 10 more people see it, then your R_0 is greater than one. If 10 people read your content and only one of them forwards it, then your R_0 is point one.

This means you want your content to be as remarkable as possible and you want to make it as easy as possible for people to spread your content through X, Facebook, LinkedIn, YouTube, Reddit, etc. Putting registration barriers in front of your content will ensure an R_0 of less than one. Setting your remarkable content free and enabling people to share it on social media sites, combined with huge reach (which we discussed), can help you get as high an R_0 as possible.

WHY *MASHABLE'S* CONTENT IS SHARED ACROSS THE WEB

Mashable is the defacto Web 2.0 and social media blog read by over 2.4 million people. Instead of putting its content behind barriers the way some mainstream media outlets do (i.e., the *Wall Street Journal*), they removed all barriers to people reading, linking to, and sharing its content with others. Prominently displayed on every blog post are *Mashable's* social-sharing buttons, including Google Buzz, X, Facebook, e-mail, and the relatively new Facebook "I Like" or "thumbs-up" button.

Mashable is particularly good about keeping up-to-date with these social sharing tools: within moments of Google announcing Google Buzz, for example, *Mashable* had the Buzz icon on every post to make it easy for readers to spread content using this new tool. Shortly after Facebook announced its "I Like" feature, *Mashable* had this button on every post.

By removing barriers to its content, making it easy to spread, and adding social sharing features as they become available, the site gets over 15 million monthly page views.

ROCK ON

Make it easy to spread your content

Whether you're just getting started in social media or you're a blackbelt, it pays to make it easy for your marketplace to spread your content for you.

ACTION: Create content that people are eager to share. This means you should focus on content that is interesting to your marketplace, don't simply talk up your own products and services.

Integrate social media throughout your marketing. If you have a blog or podcast, put social sharing buttons on each article so that it's easy for readers to help you spread your great ideas. If you create content on LinkedIn, reply to each and every comment to juice the LinkedIn algorithm to share you content more widely.

You should make it easy for people to spread your offline marketing activities as well by encouraging folks to follow you on X and Facebook on any advertising you still might be doing.

Chapter 15
Upgrade to Premium

In an era when nearly every other band had "no cameras or recording devices" printed on tickets, the Grateful Dead said "Why not?" and created a huge network of people who traded tapes in a sort of filesharing of the pre-Web days. With the rise of the Web, recordings, photos, and videos are now saved and traded via electronic downloads and social networking sites like Flickr and YouTube and as the technologies of sharing improved, the band is still happy to have Deadheads trade media and make copies for friends.

This open attitude didn't keep the band from making money on its own recordings, though. On top of encouraging fans to record its concerts and give away the music for free, the Grateful Dead also sells high-quality recordings of the best of their past concerts as well as studio recordings on their official web site (www.dead.net). Stop and think about this strategy for a moment—the band lets anyone record the show and trade the recordings with other fans. Yet, the band also sells high-quality recordings of those same shows. With around hundreds of select live shows available, spanning three decades of performances, fans are assured they will get a remastered recording without the excessive crowd noise common to the recordings made from the seats.

The millions of freely recorded live concert recordings in circulation on cassette tapes at peoples' homes, on college campuses, in cars, and for download on web sites serve to introduce people to the music of the Grateful Dead. Many of those people then want to see the band live to experience a concert for themselves. Then they want to collect some recordings, too. Because each show is different, fans enjoy having dozens or even hundreds of show recordings. Sooner or later, many fans then hear a high-quality recording and realize that a second or third generation recording made from the audience is lacking in sound quality. Those are the people who the band sells to, by offering the best quality.

> THE GRATEFUL DEAD ENCOURAGES PEOPLE TO RECORD SHOWS FOR FREE. HOWEVER, FOR THE BEST QUALITY, THE BAND SELLS HIGH-QUALITY RECORDINGS DIRECTLY.

Despite the fact that people could get their product for free, the Grateful Dead understood that there was still a demand for professional concert recordings. As technology has evolved, the band has continued to develop new products for their audience. On tours by The Dead and Furthur, fans had the opportunity to purchase a three-CD set of the concert itself, available just 15 minutes after the end of the show. The system is rather clever. Prior to the show, fans pay $20 at the merchandise table, get a wristband, and then enjoy the concert. Behind the scenes, crew members record the first CD and make 1,000 copies at the set break. Ditto for the second CD which is duplicated during the encore. Then, as the final note of the encore finishes, the third CD is created and quickly copied, and the set of CDs is packaged and rushed to the merchandise table. Eager fans trade their wristbands for CD sets.

We spoke with a fan at a Worcester, Massachusetts, show who said he bought the CD set (even though he can download the music for free at home) because he wanted to relisten to the show on his three-hour drive back to Vermont. We buy the band's recordings too, because we appreciate the high quality and professional mixing.

The 2009 Dead tour saw a new partnership with Blurb to offer an official tour book for each show. At each stop on the tour, a collectible book featuring the photography of longtime Grateful Dead photographer Jay Blakesberg (whose photos are featured in this book) is available. After the show, fans can go to Blurb.com and place an order for the book that includes photos from the show that you attended. Even though fans are snapping their own photos, many buy the book as an excellent memory of the experience.

Marketing Lesson from the Grateful Dead
Upgrade to Premium

The idea of giving something away for free to anybody who wants it and then providing a paid upgrade to a premium version is becoming increasingly common with products and services that have no distribution costs. For the Grateful Dead, the cost of allowing fans to record music and document concerts through photos and video costs the band nothing. That zero-cost distribution of free product and service is also possible with software delivered over the Web, electronic content delivered online, such as news, research reports, and data, and also services that are available via mobile applications.

> THE GRATEFUL DEAD TEACHES US THAT YOUR MOST PASSIONATE FANS WILL PAY A PREMIUM PRICE FOR THE BEST QUALITY.

The challenge in the upgrade model is to give away something that is considered valuable, and something that people will use regularly and become familiar with. It is the familiarity that grows from regular use—the Grateful Dead fan who regularly listens to recorded concerts—that generates the value and desire for the premium version of the same product or service.

This marketing strategy simply doesn't work when you provide something for free that has only limited value.

For example, an author who only provides the Table of Contents to his book for free hoping that people will want to buy the book will likely have little to show for the effort because this alone has little value. Similarly, a free software application with a feature set that is so crippled as to be of limited use will not sell more software.

FREE E-BOOK READERS AND CONTENT
(OR BUY THE BEST)

E-book devices are becoming extremely popular. While retailers Amazon, Barnes & Noble, and Borders earn revenue by selling the content for their e-readers (books, magazines, reports, and newspaper subscriptions), they also make money by selling the reading devices. According to an estimate by ZDNet, around 1.5 million Kindles have been sold through 2009 (Amazon does not release the number).

Amazon.com is also tapping into a Grateful Dead business model. Amazon.com offers completely free Kindle iPhone, iPad, and iPod touch applications. The Kindle application works just like the $249.00 reader: You either buy a book or choose one of the free selections at the Kindle Store and get it auto-delivered wirelessly to your iPhone, iPad, or iPod touch. Then the Kindle application makes it easy to read the book. You can also search and browse more than 480,000 books.

Of course, the size of an iPod is much smaller than a Kindle reading device, so many people who enjoy reading books on their iPhone or iPod touch will then become interested in the Kindle reader. And the battery power for a Kindle Reader is much greater than an iPad, so for long plane rides, you get more reading time on a single charge with the reader.

The upgrade path from free to premium ensures that many will pay the $249.00 for the larger Kindle reader with its superior functionality.

Barnes & Noble, with the Nook e-book reader introduced in late 2009, has an interesting advantage compared to online-only Amazon.com: Hundreds of physical stores located across the United States. Much like the Grateful Dead did with allowing fans to record concerts, Barnes & Noble has a clever way to introduce and sell content for the Nook to those who visit the stores. Customers may download and read e-books for free while in the store. The "Read in Store" program (with free Wi-Fi included) is similar to what people can already do in stores with print books and magazines—pull one off the shelf, plop down in a comfy chair, and read for no charge. When the customer wants to finish the book at home, it's a few clicks to make the purchase.

Both Amazon.com and Barnes & Noble have implemented smart ways to introduce people to both the content and the functionality of e-book readers. As we write this, Borders announced that it is accepting preorders for the new Kobo eReader and released its eBook store and applications powered by Kobo in a digital shop called Area-e, launching Summer 2010. We are eager to see how Borders applies marketing lessons from the Grateful Dead to launch and promote Kobo and the content to read on it.

ROCK ON

Develop a free offering

If you work in a software company, are part of an information business, or have an offering that can be delivered through the Web, you should be developing a free version and offering it on the Web with an upgrade path to a premium offering.

ACTION: Develop a free mobile application for your business.

For businesses that sell physical goods or services that cannot be delivered via the Web, you should consider developing a free mobile application. For example, Stanley Black & Decker, one of the world's largest hand-tool and power-tool manufacturers, offers a free level application on the iPhone. Consumers use the level for such things as checking if a picture is hanging straight on a wall. The premium version, of course, is a more accurate professional-grade level from Stanley Black & Decker, and you have to pay for that at your local hardware store.

CHAPTER 16
Loosen Up Your Brand

The Grateful Dead carried the love of improvisation they put into their music into many aspects of their business as well—including their branding. Album covers, backstage passes, newsletters, and posters were adorned with rich graphics dripping with color, detail, and imagery.

As with their concerts, you never knew what you were going to get when you bought an album, happened upon an ad for a concert, or received a newsletter. While the band reused certain images consistently—roses, skeletons, skulls, dancing bears, and the "Steal Your Face" logo—how these images were used varied wildly. The font and color of the band's name changed from album cover to concert poster to newsletter. Sometimes you would get a very cool album cover unlike anything you'd seen before . . . and other times you'd get something that left you thinking *huh?* and shrugging your shoulders.

The cover art for their 1978 album, *Shakedown Street*, for example, shows a cartoon scene of playful mayhem complete with people boogying in the street. Drawn by Gilbert Shelton, a well-known artist of the San Francisco underground comix scene, the cover is one of motion, a sly wink, and a joke: It's readily apparent that Shelton and the Grateful Dead had fun with this cover—one that their fans would savor in the months and years ahead. ("Shakedown Street" is also the name given to the rows of parking lot vendors you'd find at Grateful Dead shows.)

But then again, the band could produce relatively tame and understated cover art, as was the case with *The Grateful Dead Sampler* album. Also released in 1978, the LP cover features a simple pink skull on a black background.

> THE GRATEFUL DEAD CARRIED THEIR LOVE OF IMPROVISATION INTO THEIR BRANDING.

The Grateful Dead's branding, which was constantly changing and evolving, was in direct contrast to what other bands did. When bands like the Stones went on tour, they usually had a theme, which coincided with the album they were currently promoting. Branding was tightly controlled and carried through to all elements of their marketing: posters, T-shirts, stage sets, and so forth. To promote his 1987 *Never Let Me Die* album, David Bowie embarked on his Glass Spider Tour—complete with a stage set that included a huge inflatable spider web and spider.

The Grateful Dead, on the other hand, never really adhered to a promotional theme when touring. Poster art sometimes changed from show to show—even for concerts held just days apart. A poster advertising the December 12, 1970, concert at the Santa Rosa, California, fairgrounds was done in black and white and featured band members in cowboy hats, while the

December 22, 1970, poster for the show at the Sacramento, California Memorial Auditorium visually stimulated you with a yellow sunset, an orange volcano, and a blue ocean—all surrounded by a lavender border.

From a design perspective, the Grateful Dead incorporated a carefree nature in their graphics that you didn't see with other more carefully managed bands. The Grateful Dead's improvisational branding also showed that they knew their audience well—one that embraced nonconformity and free-form thinking in its art and music.

Marketing Lesson from the Grateful Dead
Loosen Up Your Brand

Too often companies hold tight to their branding. Marketing communications departments dictate how a company is to use a logo and corporate colors—with one person in a department billing him or herself as the "logo police"—and woe to anyone in the company who steps out of line. When David worked at NewsEdge Corporation, for example, a business unit displayed the company logo against a map of the world on their datasheet—a complete violation of "corporate branding guidelines." The offending product managers were taken to task, told to remove the "nonofficial" image, and to reprint their datasheets.

Of course companies need branding guidelines—we're not advocating that you do away with how and where your corporate logo is used. Holding tight to branding, however, stifles creativity. Instead of congratulating a product marketing team for taking the initiative in creating something new, the branding police clamp down—and effectively shut off new ideas.

> THE GRATEFUL DEAD TEACHES US TO SHOW OUR BRAND'S PERSONALITY AND TO TRUST THAT OUR CUSTOMERS WILL RECOGNIZE OUR BRAND EVEN IF IT LOOKS A LITTLE "DIFFERENT."

When designing your web sites, e-books, infographics, and social media profiles, give your design professionals some leeway. Yes, you want them to follow your corporate design standards, but let them deviate from those standards as appropriate. Professional designers know how to exercise their skill and incorporate fresh ideas without deviating completely from your brand.

By loosening up your brand, you allow your company to show its personality—and, by extension, its ability to roll with the punches.

GOOGLE LIGHTENS UP ITS IMAGE WITH DOODLES

One company that's passionate about protecting its logo is Google. While the company allows people to use screen shots of search results pages in their blog posts, e-books, and printed books, people cannot use the Google logo in movies or TV shows without express permission. And, use of the logo on merchandise and clothing, or third-party marketing materials such as tradeshows, is expressly forbidden.

Yet Google also has a rich tradition of modifying its logos for special events. Called "Google's Doodles," these whimsically designed logos celebrate everything from Van Gogh's birthday to the 50th anniversary of Lego. The doodles, stylized versions of the colorful Google logo used on the Web search page, frequently celebrate holidays. Halloween is a favorite. Sporting events like the Olympics and World Cup Soccer generate multiple doodles as the events play out.

When Google developed its first doodle in 1998 (a stick figure behind the second "o" in Google to commemorate the Burning Man Festival), the company had no idea how popular the doodles would become: They are now collectible items and people blog or tweet whenever a new one appears.

Rather than rein in its designers and keep them from "misusing the logo," Google has made Google's Doodles part of its brand: "While the doodle is primarily a fun way for [Google] to recognize events and notable people, it also illustrates the creative and innovative personality of [our] company," the company says on its corporate site. Google now employs a full-time design team that creates doodles for the global Google site as well as the various country sites (i.e., Google.fr, Google.cn, etc.).

Like most companies (including the Grateful Dead), Google protects its image and branding and requests that you not use their logo without asking for permission. But unlike most organizations, the company shows its personality through design the same way that the Grateful Dead does. The playfulness and confidence that's part of its corporate DNA shines through—even to the extent that you might not even recognize the logo, as was the case when Google honored Jackson Pollock's birthday. On January 28, 2009, the Google logo looked like something a two-year-old might create: a drawing full of colorful streaks and scribbles.

And, in a wonderful coincidence, Google's first chef, Charlie Ayers, was the Grateful Dead's former chef!

ROCK ON

Set your designers free

ACTION: Give your designers leeway to play with your branding elements and invite customers and followers to share their ideas.

You can maintain strict control over your brand in-house, but you quickly lose control once your brand is online. Let people use your theme song in videos and add your logo to blog posts. Instead of fighting back, post the more creative videos and other content to your web site. Or why not crowdsource the next design that you need by announcing a contest for young designers to take a crack at, say, your tradeshow booth graphics. No matter what you do with outside people, you should certainly let your in-house and chief outside designers come up with new ideas that loosen up your brand . . . while still maintaining your corporate image.

CHAPTER 17
Partner with Entrepreneurs

You can smell a Grateful Dead concert before you even enter the parking lot—the scent in the air is a weird combination of frying sausage, pot smoke, and patchouli. Then, as you open your car door, you suddenly hear it: laughter, conversations, a clash of different Grateful Dead tunes. The song "Sugar Magnolia" is playing nearby, the sound a bit tinny from the bad car stereo, but from afar "The Wheel" booms from a professional sound system that a member of the Grateful Dead tribe is running from a gas-powered generator.

You've hung out at the scene dozens of times before, always making the journey with friends. The scene is wherever the Grateful Dead is playing tonight and it may be a different city, a different parking lot, and a different afternoon, but the scene is a comfortable constant in your crazy life.

Eager to find the center of the tribe, you follow your ears and your nose and soon you see it, rows and rows of makeshift stalls. Slowly, very slowly, you and your friends walk through, saying hello to people you know. You casually handle some of the merchandise on display, not so much because you might want to buy but rather to have a quick conversation with others in the Grateful Dead community. Homemade tie-dye T-shirts, lovingly crafted macramé bracelets, and leather belts are all on offer from itinerant Dead entrepreneurs. Hungry and thirsty from the long drive, you can choose from the many food and drink stalls—burritos, grilled cheese sandwiches, or any one of a dozen varieties of beer.

Like at a Medieval Faire, the underbelly is there too: a little weed perhaps? Care for a hit of nitrous oxide from a balloon? Many of the sellers follow the band around the country, specializing in one type of product, providing the same customers with their goods at show after show.

And then there's the merchandise . . .

> **RATHER THAN SAY NO, THE GRATEFUL DEAD LICENSED THEIR LOGOS TO ENTREPRENEURS, WHO USE THEM ON MERCHANDISE THAT THEY SELL AT CONCERTS.**

Introduced after the band played Woodstock in 1969, the round red, white, and blue symbol depicting a skull with a lightning bolt bisecting the forehead was originally used as a stencil on road cases that tended to get mixed up among bands at large festival gigs. But within a decade, the "Steal Your Face" logo became one of the most recognized symbols in the world. Fans can't resist the logo and eagerly purchase stickers, shirts, coffee mugs, motorcycle jackets, pins, headbands, and dozens of other articles emblazoned with the "Stealie." A few years later, another image, the "Dancing Bears," became popular, too.

Sellers in the Grateful Dead parking lot scene were making good money on merchandise displaying the band logos, and the Grateful Dead road crew took notice. But rather than clamping down, the band brought the entrepreneurial sellers into the fold, making them partners by simply requiring a licensing fee to use the logo.

MARKETING LESSON FROM THE GRATEFUL DEAD
Partner with Entrepreneurs

Most bands prohibit the sale of merchandise in parking lots because they want to ensure that only "official" merchandise is being sold. While the Grateful Dead also sold their own gear inside, they partnered with the vendor community, resulting in some very creative uses of the logo, such as on baby clothes. In addition, the act of bringing the sellers into the fold served to keep the thriving parking lot scene intact, complete with positive vibes for all to enjoy.

> THE GRATEFUL DEAD TEACHES US TO FIND THE ENTREPRENEURS WHO WOULD LIKE TO MAKE MONEY FROM YOUR BRAND AND WORK WITH THEM TO DO SO.

The inclusive, collaborative atmosphere that is the Grateful Dead experience carried through to the independent merchandise sellers at the band's live concerts. Later, with the rise of the Web, Web sales entrepreneurs were also treated with respect and licensed to sell.

In a previous chapter, we talked about cutting out the middleman. Recall that we discussed how the Grateful Dead sold tickets directly to fans. Now in this chapter, we're suggesting that you partner with entrepreneurs in the way that the Grateful Dead did with merchandise sellers. At first glance, these strategies may seem contradictory. They're not. Instead, they are two different strategies. While ticket brokers acted as a monopoly (until the Dead broke it) and made money from tickets to the bands shows that would have sold anyway, the merchandise sellers, who were not acting as a monopoly, were adding to the availability of goods. Each style of T-shirt, coffee cup, sweatshirt, and pin was a bit different. Just as important, the ticket brokers were huge corporations, not Grateful Dead fans. The merchandise sellers were entrepreneurial fans.

AMAZON.COM:
THE WORLD'S MOST POPULAR AFFILIATE PROGRAM

Amazon.com began offering services in 1995, first as an online bookseller. Founder Jeff Bezos realized that an online bookseller could carry much more inventory than even the largest physical store. Bezos believed that only the Web could offer customers the convenience of browsing a selection of millions of book titles in a single sitting. During the first 30 days of business, Amazon.com fulfilled orders for customers in 50 states and 45 countries, all shipped from his Seattle-area garage.

Amazon.com initially operated in a relatively traditional sense. The company built a place to warehouse books, accompanied by an online storefront, selling products themselves, and the company soon started selling more than just books. Today you can buy just about anything on Amazon.com: cameras, electronics, personal care items, musical instruments, and much more. But quickly, people at Amazon.com figured out that being a lone site in the vast World Wide Web wasn't the only strategy.

Like the Grateful Dead, Amazon.com began partnering with entrepreneurs who appear, on the surface, to be competitors. The company developed two programs, an affiliate program and Amazon Associates, both at odds with what was expected at the time.

Amazon.com partners with affiliates who want to sell merchandise through the company's e-commerce platform by embedding product links or entire storefronts on affiliates' web sites or blogs. Being an Amazon affiliate means essentially that, when people become intrigued by a product that is featured or discussed on your site, you link them to the appropriate Amazon.com page to purchase it. For example, a book review blog that is an Amazon affiliate would include links to buy each book reviewed. Then, when someone buys through the link, the affiliate gets a percentage (in the range of 5 percent to 15 percent) of the revenue. That Amazon.com decided back in 2000 to allow sales from sites other than their own web site is surprising, because at the time the conventional wisdom was to "keep traffic on your own site." This was a

Grateful Dead–style move to be inclusive and include others as sellers. The affiliate program has become the largest and most popular Web affiliate program in the world.

Amazon.com also provides Amazon Associates an opportunity to sell products directly on the Amazon.com site. Wide controversy initially surrounded the ability of Amazon Associates to sell used books. The practice seems to be counterproductive because a used book might sell for one or two dollars on Amazon.com compared to the new version of the identical book for twenty dollars. Authors and publishers complained that new book sales were being cannibalized by the availability of cheaper used copies. But Amazon.com sided with the hundreds of thousands of entrepreneurs who sell used books through the site.

When the Grateful Dead began licensing sellers of logo merchandise, many observers thought the program foolish because the band was thought to be reducing its overall revenue. But band members decided it was better to get more logos out there and to keep the community happy than to make a few more dollars. They figured, rightly of course, that the money would come as the band became even more popular. For the Grateful Dead, the strategy was wildly successful. And the money certainly came for Amazon.com, too. These partnering decisions greatly contributed to spreading the word and helped turn Amazon.com into a business with 2009 net sales of $24.51 billion and net income of $902 million.

ROCK ON

Partner with those who are eager to sell your stuff

Do you have people selling versions of your products and services that seem in competition to your direct sales efforts? Maybe the right thing to do is to partner with those entrepreneurs rather than sending them a legal notice. What about companies that sell services related to yours? Is there an opportunity there?

ACTION: Get with your legal staff and make it clear that you want to review any cease-and-desist action before it is implemented. In many organizations, the initial reaction—to say "no"—is implemented before anyone has a chance to review the decision. Better yet, proactively find and approach companies that seem to be competitors and work out a way to help one another. If you're a realtor, why not forge a partnership with a home improvement company. Manufacturers or retailers of baby and children products should work out a deal to sell merchandise on so-called "Mommy-blogger" sites.

CHAPTER 18
Give Back

The Grateful Dead frequently threw their support behind causes and ideas they believed in, especially anything related to improving life in their home base of San Francisco. Starting in the 1960s, the band participated in frequent benefit concerts, donating the proceeds to support a variety of important causes. For example, an early benefit for the Haight Ashbury Legal Organization, in which the Grateful Dead and other acts performed at the Winterland Ballroom on May 30, 1966, raised $12,000 to fund legal help for those who could not afford it. Giving back to the community became an essential element of the band's brand image.

"Giving back" was not just limited to benefit concerts. At the band's regular shows, they invited favorite organizations to set up tables in the hallways and educate fans on issues like organ donation and voter registration. Concertgoers knew the Grateful Dead's commitment was authentic and that added to the perception of the band's positive and supportive approach to making music and helping people improve their lives.

> **THE GRATEFUL DEAD WAS REMARKABLY GENEROUS, A BRAND ATTRIBUTE THAT CONTRIBUTED TO THEIR GROWTH AND PROSPERITY OVER MANY YEARS.**

For nearly 20 years, the Grateful Dead organized benefit concerts as the primary vehicle for giving. But band members became increasingly overwhelmed with the sheer number of requests coming into the Grateful Dead offices and the frequent infighting among groups about how the substantial proceeds from their charitable efforts should be allocated. So in 1983, band members established the Rex Foundation (www.rexfoundation.org) as a nonprofit charitable organization to make it easier to support causes they believed in.

> The Rex Foundation aims to help secure a healthy environment, promote individuality in the arts, provide support to critical and necessary social services, assist others less fortunate than ourselves, protect the rights of indigenous people and ensure their cultural survival, build a stronger community, and educate children and adults everywhere.

The Rex Foundation enabled the Grateful Dead to better handle the countless individual requests for benefit concerts they received and, at the same time, support many more causes than they could with one-off concerts. The first benefit concerts for the Rex Foundation were held in the spring of 1984 at the Marin Veteran's Memorial Auditorium. Then, each Spring, the band did a three-night run at a venue in the San Francisco area with all profits going to the foundation. The Rex Foundation, in turn, makes grants to organizations focused on the environment (e.g., Women's Earth Alliance), human services (Hearts of Gold, for example, enhances the lives of New York City's homeless mothers and their children), and the arts (support of obscure composers such as Havergal Brian and Robert Simpson). The Grateful Dead concerts and activities have been the primary source of funds over the years, but the Rex Foundation also accepts donations from citizens and corporations. Since it was founded, the Rex Foundation has granted $8.5 million to over 1,000 recipients.

Marketing Lesson from the Grateful Dead
Give Back

While companies frequently support nonprofit charities, often these initiatives can seem more like an item on a corporate checklist or a tax write-off. It is rare when a company's support seems authentic or is a core value of the company's brand. There are many companies that give generously but don't focus efforts on one area or problem—related to their brand—that they can work toward resolving. Instead many companies make donations to a random selection of senior executives' favorite charities.

> **THE GRATEFUL DEAD TEACHES US THAT A CONSISTENT AND SUSTAINED LEVEL OF GIVING BACK TO THE COMMUNITY IS OF SIGNIFICANT BENEFIT TO COMPANIES.**

When a company carefully chooses a particular charity or cause to support and makes it a part of their corporate culture, continuing the commitment over many years, the accrued benefits to both the brand and the recipient charity can be enormous.

RONALD MCDONALD HOUSE CHARITIES

When we think of McDonald's restaurants, we think of children. Sure, the tasty food is a guilty pleasure for adults now and then too (after a Grateful Dead concert, perhaps), but what comes to mind first is kids. So we find the Ronald McDonald House Charities (www.rmhc.org), started by McDonald's Corporation in 1974, a fascinating example of Grateful Dead–style corporate giving. The organization is a nonprofit and like the Rex Foundation accepts donations from others, but McDonald's Corporation is the largest corporate donor.

The organization was established to help families who travel far from home to get treatment for their seriously ill or injured children. Recognizing the stress and pain within families when children are away from home for long periods of time, the initial house in Philadelphia was founded, and the project has grown to nearly 300 Ronald McDonald Houses in 30 countries, offering families a way to stay together near treatment hospitals. Ronald McDonald Houses serve more than 10,000 families each day and, in 2008, saved families more than $226 million in hotel costs. The charity has expanded to also include the Ronald McDonald Family Room (a special room for families located within hospitals) and the Ronald McDonald Care Mobile (a fully staffed mobile pediatric health care facility offering services to children).

> The mission of Ronald McDonald House Charities is to create, find, and support programs that directly improve the health and well-being of children.

If you've ever been in a hospital, you can relate to how afraid a child would be if left there alone and the importance of having family nearby. That's why this is a great way to give back—people remember the effort, it is consistent with the family orientation of the company, and it has been sustained over more than three decades.

ROCK ON

Give back to your community

Of course most of us don't have the ability to perform benefit concerts in front of 20,000 people, nor are we likely to work within a huge company that can invest in a Ronald McDonald's House–sized effort. Don't let that stop you from giving back! Follow the lead of the Grateful Dead and give back in your area of expertise. For example, we frequently speak as guest lecturers at colleges and universities in the Boston area. We feel that providing our ideas to students at Harvard, MIT, Boston University, Simmons, Babson, Emerson, and other institutions is a worthwhile way for us to personally give back to our community. It not only benefits the students but positively benefits us too.

ACTION: Pick a way to give back to your community in some form that is consistent with your brand and start doing it now.

Chapter 19
Do What You Love

In preparing to write this book, we both watched lots of footage of the Grateful Dead. One thing that stood out was how happy Jerry Garcia was on stage—he had a big smile on his face while his fingers danced up and down his guitar fret. Similarly, when we listened to interviews of him and other members of the band, they often talked about how they *loved* what they did. This passion helped them overcome serious odds to become a huge success.

As is often the case for people starting out in a career pursuing their passion, some of the Grateful Dead members had *very* humble beginnings. Jerry Garcia, for example, was really passionate about music and playing guitar, so much so that prior to starting the band, he was a guitar teacher making such meager wages that he had to live out of his car! Rather than get a "job," he stuck with it, and his passion fueled his eventual success.

BECAUSE THE GRATEFUL DEAD LOVED WHAT THEY DID, THEY STUCK WITH IT AND (OBVIOUSLY) EVENTUALLY PROSPERED.

Since they were so passionate about what they did, the Grateful Dead were also able to persevere through some very rough times. On the first gig they booked, they were contracted for performances two nights in a row. They were so bad the first night that the owner of the joint replaced them with three elderly gentlemen in a jazz band! The band members were so embarrassed they didn't even bother asking the owner for their one night's pay. Rather than throw up their hands and give up, the band went back to the studio and doubled down on the practice routines. It actually took several years and a great deal of practice before they really started getting good market traction with their unique sound.

Marketing Lesson from the Grateful Dead
Do What You Love

We are taught as children that work and play are opposing forces in nature. This teaching is incorrect—it *is* possible that your work can be like play! In fact, if you do what you love the way the Grateful did, you'll never "work" a day in your life.

People often end up in "jobs" they're not passionate about because they're living someone else's dream—their mother-in-law's, their competitive sister's, their classmate's, and so forth. It is *much* easier to succeed at fulfilling your own dreams for which you have passion than it is to fulfill others' dreams—this is because you're much more likely to do *great* work if you're doing what you love. When others get tired in your industry, your passion will act like jet fuel to help you overcome barriers that they can't. You're *much* better off working in an industry in decline that you're passionate about (i.e., even the car business) than you are working in a hot, growing industry for which you have no passion (i.e., management consulting).

Not only does doing what you love increase your odds of success, but it dramatically increases your happiness. You spend more than 50 percent of your waking adult life working, so you might as well do what you love. Doing something you don't enjoy during more than 50 percent of your waking adult life takes a toll on your psyche that goes well beyond the boundaries of the workplace. Conversely, doing what you love pays huge dividends in your personal life.

> THE GRATEFUL DEAD TEACH US TO LIVE OUR OWN DREAMS—NOT SOMEONE ELSE'S.

In the months and weeks leading up to Brian's father's death, Brian saw him searching to derive meaning from his life and to put his time on Earth into a broader historical context. Fortunately, his dad lived a great life full of accomplishment and love, so it wasn't hard for him. Like Brian's father, you want those self-conversations at the end of your life to be as fruitful as possible. You'll never regret on your deathbed that you pursued your passion. However, you may regret spending half of your waking life in a dead-end job or living someone else's dream.

BILL GATES TAKES CONTROL OF HIS LIFE

Some people love Bill Gates and some people hate him. Either way, you have to admire how the guy takes control of his life and follows his passions. As a young boy, Gates was geeked out about computers. He and his friend Paul Allen (who was to be cofounder of Microsoft) spent countless hours in the middle of the night at the University of Washington using the university's mainframe computers—which must have disappointed his father, a prominent Seattle lawyer who hoped his son would follow him into the law.

Gates brought his passion with him to Harvard, where he continued to tinker with computers along with Allen. He started doing some consulting work on the side and eventually dropped out of Harvard to found Microsoft and pursue his passion full time. The rest of the story is well-worn history, as Gates eventually became the richest man in the world by doing what he loved.

After over 30 years at Microsoft and while still a relatively young man, Gates decided to retire and pursue a new passion. He and his wife, Melinda, started the Bill & Melinda Gates Foundation, which is dedicated to bringing innovations in health and learning to developing countries. By following this second passion, he has helped countless children in developing countries improve their lives.

ROCK ON

Carpe diem!

Like the Grateful Dead and Bill Gates have done before you, follow your passion and you'll be rewarded in spades.

ACTION: If you hate your "job," start work to change it today. Stop complaining and start doing something. For example, if you're reading this book, you're probably a marketing geek, business executive, or entrepreneur. Like us, you have a different vision of how marketing should be done by your company, and you have ideas on how to transform your industry. Put together a presentation on how you want to take your "job" in a new direction that will help transform the way your company markets itself. If you need more help on doing this, read our other books, *The New Rules of Marketing & PR* and *Inbound Marketing*.

If turning your job into something you're passionate about doesn't work in two months, then look for a new "passion." (Change the word "job" for "passion"—it helps!) While searching for your new "passion," turn the process on its head. Don't go through the job boards looking for another job. Target companies and industries you're excited about and sell them on creating a new position for you around your "passion." Write letters to CEOs and attach your PowerPoint slide deck or brilliant blog article about how you would transform their business if the company hired you—any CEO worth her salt would take that meeting.

If you have an idea for a new company burning a hole in the back of your head, start working on it during nights and weekends—this is how many businesses start. As you get some traction, go for it. It's less risky than you think.

Here we are, two Grateful Dead fans, and we're actually writing a book about the band. Is this work? Well, yeah. But it is also our passion. We're living our dream.

As Walt Disney said, "All our dreams can come true, if we have the courage to pursue them."

Acknowledgments

The authors would like to thank
Our friends at John Wiley & Sons, including Shannon Vargo, Zach Schisgal, and Amanda Pyne. Thanks to Doug Eymer for the awesome book design, Jay Blakesberg for the photos, and Richard Biffle for the illustrations. A huge thank you to Bill Walton for sharing his passion for the Grateful Dead with us in the Foreword.

Brian would like to thank
Dharmesh Shah, Ray Ozzie, Bill Walton, Tom Hamilton, Nick Swift, Jerry Garcia, Eric Olsen, Bob Halligan.

David would like to thank
Yukari Watanabe Scott, Allison Goulet-Scott, Ben Goulet-Scott, Alan Scott, Peter Scott, Jim Parmele, Mason Tolman, Paul Sherbine, Berkeley Johnson, Bill Merikallio, Mark Reiss, Juanito Pascual, Andy Logan, Nate Bidner, Jason Scheuner, Meredith Christensen, and TJ Kanczuzewski.

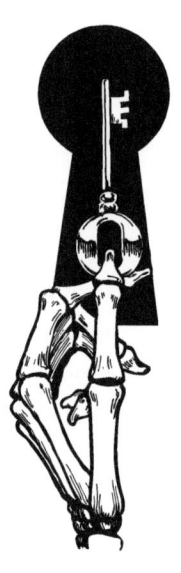

"Furthur" Reading

While researching this book, the following sources were invaluable to us.

Books

A Long Strange Trip: The Inside History of the Grateful Dead, by Dennis McNally. Broadway Books, 2002.

Between the Dark and Light: The Grateful Dead Photography of Jay Blakesberg, by Jay Blakesberg with a foreword by Phil Lesh. Backbeat Books, 2002.

Garcia: A Signpost to New Space, by Jerry Garcia, Charles Reich, and Jann Wenner. Da Capo Press, 2003.

Searching for the Sound: My Life with the Grateful Dead, by Phil Lesh. Little, Brown, 2005.

Grateful Dead: The Illustrated Trip. DK Books, 2003.

Living with the Dead: Twenty Years on the Bus with Garcia and the Grateful Dead, by Rock Scully. Cooper Square Press, 2001.

Home Before Daylight: My Life on the Road with the Grateful Dead, by Steve Parish. St. Martin's Press, 2003.

Magazine Articles

"How to 'Truck' the Brand: Lessons from the Grateful Dead," by Glenn Rifkin. *strategy+business,* first quarter, 1997.

"Management Secrets of the Grateful Dead," by Joshua Green. *The Atlantic,* March 2010.

Web Sites

"7 Business Lessons I Learned From The Grateful Dead," by Rob Kelly. www.purchase.com, accessed April 4, 2010.

The official site of the Grateful Dead: www.dead.net.

About the Photographs

The remarkable photographs in this book are the work of Jay Blakesberg, a San Francisco-based photographer whose work has appeared in many magazines, books, documentary films, and record industry packaging.

Blakesberg began photographing the Grateful Dead when he was a high school student in 1978 and soon joined the traveling caravan that followed the band from city to city. In later years he began working closely with the band and was given access to create more intimate and exclusive images.

Over the past 48 years his photographic rock 'n' roll journey has included work with many legendary artists, such as Carlos Santana, Tom Waits, Neil Young, Joni Mitchell, Radiohead, Phish and the Grateful Dead to name just a few. Recently his work has been the subject of three major museum retrospectives.

Follow along on Instagram @retroblakesberg and @jayblakesberg

About the Illustrations

The amazing original illustrations in the book are by Richard Biffle, an artist whose mystical fantasy pieces inspire many minds. For decades, Biffle has been working with the Grateful Dead (as well as the individual band member's spinoff projects), creating the fantastic artwork seen on Grateful Dead posters, merchandise, and CD covers.

Biffle has worked with many different bands besides the Grateful Dead, including Santana, the Black Crowes, the Allman Brothers Band, Crosby, Stills, Nash & Young, Paul Simon, Deep Purple, and many more. His art outside the music industry includes work with Marvel Comics.

Connect with him on the Web at www.richardbiffle.com.

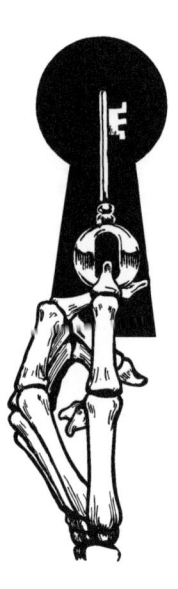

About the Authors

Brian Halligan

Brian coined the term Inbound Marketing and started the movement around Inbound Marketing, which was at least partially inspired by watching the way the Grateful Dead went about marketing themselves. Brian then co-founded HubSpot as a modern software platform to enable companies to go to market in a way that was inspired by the Grateful Dead. He was CEO of HubSpot from $0 to $25billion. During that time, he was a frequent flyer on the lists of best CEOs.

Brian developed MIT's popular Scaling Entrepreneurial Ventures class, which he has taught for over a decade. In recognition of his outstanding mentorship in entrepreneurship, MIT Sloan honored Brian with the Monosson Prize. Brian is also a senior advisor at Sequoia Capital, where he coaches startup founders on their journey to becoming scaleup CEOs.

As the founder of Propeller Ventures, Brian directs a $100 million climate tech venture fund, specializing in ocean innovation investments.

Brian's the proud owner and steward of Jerry Garcia's Wolf guitar which he lets intrepid artists such as John Mayer, Tom Hamilton and Nick Swift play often. Currently, Brian is working on a film that explores the life and times of John Perry Barlow, writer of 30 Grateful Dead songs. He is also a co-author of an upcoming Harvard Business Review case study on the Grateful Dead.

 About the Authors

David Meerman Scott

Since his first Grateful Dead show when he was a teenager in 1979, David Meerman Scott has seen the band perform over 100 times.

David is a marketing strategist and a professional speaker. He is the author of the *BusinessWeek* bestselling book *The New Rules of Marketing & PR,* the *Wall Street Journal* bestseller *Fanocracy* and several other books. He speaks at conferences and corporate events around the world. He loves to dance the Lindy Hop (but isn't very good at it), collects artifacts from the Apollo lunar program, and maintains a database, with 1016 entries at this writing, of every concert he has attended since 1976. He is a graduate of Kenyon College where he listened to a heck of a lot of Grateful Dead in his dorm room.

Learn more at www.DavidMeermanScott.com

Authors David Meerman Scott (left) and Brian Halligan (right).